INGEBORG BACHMANN was born in 1926 in Klagenfurt, Austria. She studied philosophy at the universities of Innsbruck, Graz, and Vienna, where she wrote her dissertation on Martin Heidegger. In 1953 she received the poetry prize from Gruppe 47 for her first volume, *Borrowed Time* (*Die gestundete Zeit*), after which there followed her second collection, *Invocation of the Great Bear* (*Anrufung des Großen Bären*), in 1956. Her various awards include the Georg Büchner Prize, the Berlin Critics Prize, the Bremen Award, and the Austrian State Prize for Literature. Writing and publishing essays, opera libretti, short stories, and a novel as well, she divided her time between Munich, Zurich, and Rome, where she died in a fire in her apartment in 1973.

PETER FILKINS is an American poet whose poems, translations, and reviews have appeared in *Agni*, *The American Poetry Review*, *The American Scholar*, *Partisan Review*, *Translation*, *TriQuarterly*, and numerous other journals. He is a graduate of Williams College and Columbia University, and has studied at the University of Vienna with the support of a Fulbright grant. Since 1988, he has taught at Simon's Rock College of Bard in Great Barrington, Massachusetts.

CHARLES SIMIC was awarded the Pulitzer Prize in Poetry in 1990. He has published fifteen books of poetry, four books of prose, and numerous translations. He teaches American Literature at the University of New Hampshire.

SONGS IN FLIGHT

THE COLLECTED POEMS OF
INGEBORG BACHMANN

Translated & Introduced by
Peter Filkins

Foreword by
Charles Simic

Marsilio Publishers
New York

The following translations have appeared in the periodicals listed, some of them in slightly different form:

The American Poetry Review — "After This Flood," "Shadows, Roses Shadow," "The Native Land," "In the Storm of Roses," "Early Noon," "March Stars".
Paris Review — "Letter in Two Drafts," "In Apulia".
Sulfur — "In Twilight," "Psalm".
The Massachusetts Review — "Borrowed Time".
TriQuarterly — "Every Day," "No Delicacies".
Partisan Review — "A Type of Loss".
Ironwood — "Journey Out".
Translation — "Invocation of the Great Bear," "My Bird," "Rome at Night," "Wood and Shavings".
The Bloomsbury Review — "Exile".
Poetry East — "Message".
Visions-International — "Paris".

CONTENTS

Early and Late Poems

Foreword by

Charles Simic

> I am a dead man who wanders
> registered nowhere

I first read Ingeborg Bachmann some thirty years ago in Jerome Rothenberg's small anthology of young German poets. I liked her poems immediately, even though Hans Magnus Enzensberger, Paul Celan and Günter Grass with their radical imagery suited my taste for novelty much more. In fact, there was nothing obviously modern about Bachmann's poems if one thinks of modernism as a tradition that includes Expressionism, Dada and Surrealism. Such poems tend to be programatically irreverent and anti-poetic. In contrast, Bachmann wrote in a manner that would not have seemed entirely unfamiliar to the great Romantic poets, that is, until they started reading her closely and realized her profound difference.

I myself remember being made uneasy even at my first encounter. Here was a poetry of sublime lyricism that suggested the knowledge of the horrors of the Second World War without employing any of its familiar images. Bachmann had a way of writing about nature such that it reminded one of concentration camps, as it were. In every new anthology of German poetry that subsequently came out, I sought her out, and when I did find the same few poems that kept being translated over and over again, I experienced once more her spell. Very simply, I knew that I had just read a poet that I would never forget.

This is one of the true mysteries of literature. What is it that makes certain poems immediately memorable? Obviously, it could be the sheer mastery of form and originality of the imagination that captivate us. Still, this is not always an explanation. Tastes change,

newness wears out. Poems that once seemed unforgettable because
of their shocking imagery or content suddenly cease to seduce us.
Long after the dazzling virtuosity of one kind or another, the
absence of something far more important becomes noticeable. I
have here in mind that elusive property known as the poet's voice.
In the case of Bachmann, it is not so much what she says, or even
how she says it, rather, it is her voice that one always remembers. A
voice that touches the heart. One could go so far as to claim that the
sound of a living voice is all that lyric poetry conveys.

The voice is the imprint of individuality. The tone of one's voice,
as everybody knows, varies depending on the attitude one takes
toward the words one is saying. In poetry, it is the voice that brings
the breath of the living human being to us. The tone either per-
suades us that what is being said matters, or it does not, and that
tone cannot be contrived. Here's someone bearing witness to her
consciousness and the wonder of its existence. The world is a strange
place, and what is even more strange is that I should be alive in it
today! No grammar of that sensation is possible, as Emily Dickinson
knew. She also understood that poets aim to recreate in their poems
the feel of that *something* which cannot be put into words.

The preoccupation of so much post-1945 poetry in Germany and
elsewhere is language. Are there any words still left around that one
can trust? It is the weight of the unsayable that gives Bachmann's
poetry its tragic dimension.

> Where Germany's earth blackens the sky,
> a cloud seeks words and fills the crater with silence.

She takes into account the profound philosophical and moral
difficulty of being a poet in an epoch of history's greatest murderers,
an epoch furthermore in which whatever explanations of evil we
once turned to for solace have become inadequate. The death of
God, you may say, is no big deal if everybody behaves well, but once

the slaughter of the innocent starts, how do you catch any sleep at
night? An air of permanent crises and terror surrounding all human
endeavor is our inheritance.

> War is no longer declared,
> but rather continued. The outrageous
> has become the everyday. The hero
> is absent from the battle. The weak
> are moved into the firing zone.
> The uniform of the day is patience,
> the order of merit is the wretched star
> of hope over the heart.

If that was all there was to it, our predicament would be far more
clear. But, there is another paradox. Yes, unimaginable crimes and
sufferings have occured, and yes, the world is still beautiful. There
are still trees, lovers and children and they go about their business as
if nothing had happened. After all the nightmares and gloomy
thoughts one has had, it is astonishing to find innocence. Is it possi-
ble to be happy in a world that has seen such horrors, Bachmann
continuously asks herself? Does that knowledge always doom one to
despair and the inability to relish life for what it is?

> I am the child of great fear for the world,
> who within peace and joy hangs suspended
> like the stroke of a bell in the day's passing
> and like the scythe in the ripe pasture.

> I am the Continual-Thought-Of-Dying.

Bachmann's is a poetry of estrangement and nostalgia. Her poems
are elegies for a loss beyond words. She is the one made stranger in
the midst of her own people by that knowledge, the one condemned

to remain forever standing on the threshold. "Our Godhead, History, has ordered for us a grave from which there's no resurrection" she says. Her poems have an awareness of the tragic worthy of the Greeks. She is the poet of the long, dark night of history and the lone human being awake in it. It is her heroic refusal to make things intellectually and morally easy for herself that gives her poems the heroic stature and nobility they have.

In a century of displaced persons, Bachmann's poetry, appropriately, is full of voyages and partings. This prodigal daughter knows that we cannot ever say what our fates truly mean; we can only try to convey endlessly how things appear to us. Every day we say farewell to some small epiphany that made the world so vivid and meaningful yesterday. Whoever in the future wishes to experience that all-pervading sense of exile our age has felt, should read Bachmann, just as we must be immensely grateful that Peter Filkins has now given us the fullest and the best translation we have in English of this magnificent poet.

ON THE BORDER OF SPEECH

Peter Filkins

When Yeats wrote in *A Vision* of the urge "to hold in a single thought reality and justice," he could just as well have been describing the impetus behind the poetry of Ingeborg Bachmann. Bridging the poetry of experience and the poetry of ideas, Bachmann's vision is one continually fixed upon the terror she perceived within the quotidian, as well as the need to elicit the unspoken, primeval truth that lies just beyond the pale of the "unspeakable." In following this trajectory, Bachmann's poems conduct a journey *in* thought *towards* feeling, for hers is not a poetry of recollected experience, nor a poetry of ideas about experience, but rather a poetry that enacts *the experience of ideas* in order to evoke the nature of true feeling, despite the impediments that exist in cognitive speech.

Born on June 25, 1926, Bachmann grew up in Klagenfurt, Austria, the eldest of three children. Capital of Carinthia, the country's most southern province, Klagenfurt is situated in a deep valley at the foot of rugged, snow-capped mountains that provide the natural borders between three countries – Austria, Yugoslavia, and Italy. Though Bachmann spent her entire adult life living away from the sleepy provincial city, her childhood in Klagenfurt remained a lasting influence. Its fields, lakes, and forest paths continually appear in her work, and it was also there that Bachmann first encountered the brutality of the "real" world when, at the age of twelve, she stood with her family as they watched Hitler and his troops march triumphant into the main square of the city in 1938. Years later, Bachmann would maintain that this moment marked the end of her childhood, a world of innocence shattered by the brutality that the young girl perceived in the marching troops and the hysteria that welcomed them.[1]

In fact, the border drawn between Bachmann and her childhood on that day became the central obsession of her imaginative life. Because of the fear that stirred in her, the border between the real and the imagined, as well as the struggle to cross it through language, became "not a problem of logic, but rather a question of existence."[2] Bachmann herself locates this dilemma in the historical terrain of Klagenfurt, for in a short biographical piece found among her papers after her death, she writes:

> I spent my childhood in Carinthia, in the South, on the border, in a valley that had two names — one German and the other Slovenian. And the house in which for generations my ancestors had lived — both Austrians and Wends — still bears a name that sounds foreign. Hence, near the border there is still another border: the border of speech — and on either side I was accustomed to stories of good and bad spirits from two or three lands; for an hour away, over the mountains, there also lay Italy.[3]

Thus, whether traveling between the focal points of innocence and guilt, hope and despair, life and death, Bachmann's poetic journey is both localized and universal. In confronting the "border of speech" that she found erected all about her in childhood, as well as the threat of those marching troops, Bachmann encountered early on the duality of "the unspeakable" as a realm of both "good and bad spirits," the need to elicit each through the urge to cross over into "the spoken" becoming the central vector of her adult life and work.

That vector was to travel swiftly, for Bachmann's rise to prominence in German letters was meteoric. After studying briefly at the universities of Graz and Innsbruck during the war, she transferred to the University of Vienna, where in 1950 she completed a doctoral thesis on "Die kritische Aufnahme der Existentialphilosophie Martin Heideggers" ("The Critical Reception of the Existential Philosophy of Martin Heidegger"). While employed at Radio Rot-Weiß-Rot in Vienna, in 1952 Bachmann first traveled to Munich to read at the influential gathering of post-war German writers known as Gruppe 47. The poet Paul Celan, whom she had met in Vienna, was instrumental in arranging her appearance, and though the recital of his "Todesfuge" was a stunning event, Bachmann's own reading was lauded with praise and awe. The German literary world was immediately swept away by the young blond-haired poet reading her poems in a near whisper, and soon her work appeared in leading journals. The following year Bachmann's first collection, *Die gestundete Zeit* (*Borrowed Time*) was published, and at the age of twenty seven she returned to the congress to receive the coveted Gruppe 47 Prize amid torrents of acclaim.

Bachmann's early success was instantaneous, landing her on the cover of *Der Spiegel* in 1954. She also soon found herself swamped with requests for poems, radio plays, and opera libretti, these being the genres that she continued to work in throughout the 1950's. Traveling to the United States in 1955 at the invitation of Harvard University, publishing her second volume of poems, *Anrufung des Großen Bären* (*Invocation of the Great Bear*) in 1956, and invited to deliver the inaugural lectures for the poetry chair founded at Frankfurt University in 1959, Bachmann was not only the most celebrated writer of the post-war generation, but also was described as the most important German poet since Gottfried Benn.

The reasons for Bachmann's swift rise to fame are both literary and historical. Amid the devastation left behind by the war, Bachmann's poems spoke directly to a historical sense of guilt and despair, while also refusing to see the present as any better. Rather, despite Germany's burgeoning economic "miracle," here was a young poet announcing that "Harder days are coming," and that

"The loan of borrowed time/ will be due on the horizon"
("Borrowed Time").4 Furthermore, the breadth of her range as a
poet deeply connected to the classical tradition of Goethe and
Hölderlin also enabled her to boldly say that,

> Where Germany's sky blackens the earth,
> its beheaded angel seeks a grave for hate
> and offers you the bowl of the heart,
> > ("Early Noon")

and then quickly follow it with echoes of Goethe's "Der König in
Thule," as well as Schubert's *Die Winterreise* in the same poem:

> Seven years later
> it occurs to you again,
> at the fountain before the portal,
> don't look too deep within,
> as your eyes fill with tears.
>
> Seven years later,
> inside a mortuary,
> the hangmen of yesterday
> drain the golden cup.
> Your eyes lower in shame.

The result is a double sense of time, one that was contemporaneous
with Austria's recent history under fascism, as well as a broader,
more pervasive sense of time, the latter being the "historical sense"
that T.S. Eliot described as "a perception, not only of the pastness of
the past, but of its presence."

This quality alone qualifies Bachmann as one of the first poets to
successfully introduce modernism to German poetry, but if this
were the entire scope of her achievement, her work would be only a

footnote to a movement whose heyday had passed. Instead, Bachmann's vision and career are more complex, harder to pin down, if only because of the fragmentary nature of each. Hers is a voice that speaks beyond its time as much as directly to it, for throughout Bachmann's work the problem of language lifts her writing beyond the breakthroughs of modernism towards a new conception of language that, as Sabine Gölz has observed, "uses the remembrance of the past not to make it return in the same shape but repeats it in order to make something new appear"[5]

The influence of Ludwig Wittgenstein's philosophy is central to this new conception, for Bachmann continually refers to it in her writing.[6] The last sentence of Wittgenstein's *Tractatus*, "What we cannot speak about we must pass over in silence,"[7] serves as a kind of touchstone in her work, though the problem that Wittgenstein sees in the inability of language to name the "unspeakable" truth is not one that she is content to treat as unsolvable. Rather, at the end of her first essay on Wittgenstein, published in 1953, she wonders, "Or could he mean that we've squandered our language because it contains no word that can touch upon what cannot be spoken?"[8]

The question is an important one, for simply by asking it Bachmann opens up the possibility that, if the right word were to exist or be found, "the unspeakable" might be recovered as a source for "true" speech, thus helping to cleanse language of the imprecision and corruption that cause meaningful speech to be lost or misused. In post-war Germany, this was a particularly important concern for the writers of Gruppe 47 who sought to free language of the fascist overtones that still clung to it, while because of the cataclysm they had experienced, there was also a distinct distaste for the "beautiful" words of the patriotic "Blut und Boden" writings that had appeared under the Nazis. Bachmann was the first poet to come along whose "simplicity of word choice and complexity of meaning"[9] created a poetry that could forward an intelligent philosophy of language on historical terms, but with the recognition that "No country and no group, no idea, can found itself upon the reality of those [the victims] who have died."[10]

This allows Bachmann to face history head on, its "Message" being as hopeless as it is unwavering:

> Out of the corpse-warm foyer of the sky steps the sun.
> There it is not the immortals,
> but rather the fallen, we perceive.
>
> And brilliance doesn't trouble itself with decay.
> Our Godhead, History, has ordered for us a grave
> from which there is no resurrection.

What distinguishes her vision, however, from the merely apocalyptic is the intelligence and control with which she wields it, for in the perception of "the fallen," one also has the sense of a larger fall having occurred, one that implicates the viewer ("History has ordered for *us* a grave") as much as the viewed. Bachmann's approach, then, is seated within history, as well as outside it. Most often she will attest to a statement such as "Germany's sky blackens the earth" ("Early Noon") by suddenly observing that "A handful of pain vanishes over the hill," the emblematic nature of her imagery bordering on the surreal, but only for the purpose of constructing a mythos in which, at the end of the same poem, "The unspeakable passes, barely spoken, over the land."

Key to this aesthetic is Bachmann's continual employment of linguistic "fragments" *(Scherben)* to construct poems that function as mosaics.[11] In "Great Landscape Near Vienna," for instance, Bachmann describes the oil fields that mercilessly "pump/ spring from the fields." She then switches to Vienna's *Prater* and the famed ferris wheel that "trails the coat that covered our love," only to shift the focus once more outside the city when she reminds us that

Where the crane completes
its circle amid the rushes of the marsh's flat water,
on a reed the hour strikes more resonantly than waves.

Yet, as if this were not enough, we are then given a single line,
"Asia's breath lies beyond the river," Bachmann providing neither
context nor meaning for it. The effect is both eerie and chilling, for
it transports us to a larger dimension, one that sees the boundaries of
time and space as transparent demarcations. Similarly, by the end of
the poem, after musing about an array of subjects ranging from "the
theater of many peopled grief" existing in the Roman settlements
upon which Vienna is built, to the fact that "no one is saved, many
are stricken" in the present day, Bachmann can speak to the imme-
diate decay created by the threat she sees in the oil fields, but in a
manner that is timeless in its implications:

And so the fish are also dead and float
towards the black seas that await us.
But we were washed away long ago, gripped
by the pull of other streams, where the world
failed to surface and there was little cheer.
The towers of the plain sing our praises,
because we unconsciously came, falling on the rungs
of depression, then falling deeper,
with an ear sharply tuned for the fall.

Given this range, the most compelling aspect of Bachmann's
poems is that the reader may often be inclined to wonder about the
where and the *when* of any poem, but never the *who*, for the conti-
nuity of Bachmann's voice is the central source of her poetic author-
ity. "In each of my moments, I'm aware of a strange/ moment,"
says Prince Myshkin in her monologue for him, echoing the way in
which Bachmann speaks on several different planes at the same

time. However, throughout her work the localities of place and time are seated within the observing self that names them. In "The Native Land," for instance, the speaker says,

> And when I drank of myself
> and my native land
> rocked with earthquakes,
> I opened my eyes to see.
>
> Then life fell to me.

However, Bachmann displays how the observation of the I *observing* is what defines the "place" of the poem when at the end she notes:

> There the stone is not dead.
> The wick flares
> when lit by a glance.

What's important about this is that, though Bachmann often seems to border on a confessional tone in lines like "It was not you I lost,/ but the world" ("A Type of Loss") or "These days I feel no pain/ that I can forget" ("Days in White"), it is the voice of an emblematic "I," one that can even be read as a specifically feminine voice speaking to and from within a patriarchy, but more importantly which resides in a particular way of seeing, rather than in a particular self that sees. The third of Bachmann's Frankfurt lectures is, in fact, entirely devoted to a discussion of "the writing I" as a literary construct. There she argues that the "I" no longer exists within history, but that "history exists in the I,"[12] an idea perhaps as applicable to a reading of our own "confessionalist" poets as it is crucial to an understanding of how Bachmann seizes control of the self by constructing a vision where "The wick flares/ when lit by a glance" rather than the other way around.

Because the act of "seeing" has no end in itself, it lends itself to the timeless and the utopian. However, when this act is performed in and through words, it encounters the "border of speech," such that another of Wittgenstein's better known propositions in the *Tractatus*, "The limits of my language mean the limits of my world,"[13] can be read for the contrary implications of freedom and impediment that it posits. Language *is* the world in this formulation, though Bachmann was also quick to value the possibility inherent in Wittgenstein's thought that "There are, indeed, things that cannot be put into words. They *make themselves manifest.* They are what is mystical."[14] For her, the effort to evoke the mystical side of "the unspoken" in contrast to the historically "unspeakable" involves the utopian pursuit of a truth that is both transient and real. What complicates her vision, however, is her recogniton, as she argued in writing on Robert Musil, that "utopia is not an end, but rather a tendency" for the writer.[15] Thus, Bachmann's poems remain *in pursuit* of the truth, both historical and ideal, but while standing *on* the "border of speech," caught between the actual and the possible.

The two central metaphors for this pursuit are The Fall and Flight. The first, of course, has long been a traditional symbol for the expulsion from paradise into the transitory realm of human experience, and Bachmann often ascribes it to the suffering endured or caused by "the fallen" in history. The motion of Flight, however, remains a condition of transit for Bachmann, a desire for reprieve that, almost by definition, cannot end or be fulfilled. In "Night Flight," for instance, the poet is careful to describe the journey as an incomplete process, Flight versus *The* Flight, where

> We have taken off from a port
> where the return doesn't matter,
> nor the cargo, nor the haul...

We have taken off, and the cloisters are empty,
since we endure, an order that can't heal or teach.

This is why Bachmann's poems remain "songs" that are "*in* flight,"
refugees in search of refuge, but never abandoning their need for
transport in order to preserve autonomy.

This is especially true in Bachmann's second volume, where the
middle section of the long poem, "Of a Land, a River and Lakes,"
informs us about of the ideal she wishes to maintain:

And yet we are determined to speak across borders,
even if borders pass through every word:
in longing still for home, we will cross over,
and again with every place stand in accord.

Central to this passage is the rhyme in German of "Wort" and
"Ort," i.e. "word" and "place," the latter contained within the for-
mer. The bridge between the two is the "border" that Bachmann
wishes to cross, though the stanza that precedes this one lays down
the actual case at hand:

To stay together, each must feel separation;
within the same air, he feels the same split within.
Only the borders of air and the borders of green
can be healed at night by each step of the wind.

Hence, despite all efforts, the border remains intact between peo-
ple, and in a specifically tragic manner between lovers. Bachmann
recognizes this, but it never stops her from trying to lift her voice in
the attempt to cross over, whether it be in speaking to the stars
themselves in "Invocation of the Great Bear," or to the hope, in
"Songs from an Island," for a realm beyond the limits of this life,
where

When you rise again,
when I rise again,
the hangman hangs on the gate,
the hammer sinks in the sea.

Language, however, possesses its own "hammer" of order and cognition limiting the means by which it can address the "unspeakable." Increasingly, Bachmann came to struggle with this limitation at the same time that she sought to reshape and overcome it. The most significant step she made in this process was her switch to prose in mid-career, for as early as 1957, Bachmann essentially stopped writing poetry. There are eighteen more poems that were published in journals after her second and last volume, but without the singular vision and thematic organization of a succinct creative period, they function more as a transparent commentary on the development of her thought and work, much like the early poems that precede her first collection.[16]

On the other hand, Bachmann's turn to prose as the primary means with which to attack the "border of speech" was for a long time a real stumbling block in the critical reception of her work. A collection of short stories, *Das dreißigste Jahr* (*The Thirtieth Year*) appeared in 1961, bringing with it a mixture of luke warm praise and consternation as to why one of the German language's leading poets had turned to a different genre. Nonetheless, Bachmann continued to write stories and essays while declaring openly that she no longer expected or even wished to write any more poems.

Eventually the public came to accept this, even though Bachmann almost disappeared from Germany's literary scene during the sixties, an obscurity heightened by her many moves between Naples, the island of Ischia, Munich, Berlin, and Zurich, before she permanently settled in Rome. Her novel *Malina*, however, was a popular success when it appeared in 1971 as the first entry into what was planned as a trilogy of novels called *Todesarten* (*Ways of Dying*).

Another collection of stories, *Simultan* (*Simultaneous*, but available in English as *Three Paths to the Lake*), was also well received upon publication in 1972. In fact, Bachmann soon became better known, more closely studied, for her prose than she was for her poetry. Not only did the growing women's movement find in her work a voice for their issues, but readers as a whole became interested in her stark portrayal of contemporary men and women locked in the struggle between the diseases of society and the wounds of the private soul, language existing between as both scalpel and sword.

Yet the question still remains: why did Bachmann stop writing poetry? That she had said all she had to say within it is, of course, the most viable answer, yet there are few easy answers in the work of this writer. Rather, one could argue that the fragmentation of Bachmann's career, namely her success in no less than six different genres – poetry, the short story, the novel, the essay, opera libretti, and radio plays – corresponds to a major strategy of the poetry in its use of "fragments" welded into mosaic patterns by the silence they seek to break. Put another way, Bachmann's turn towards prose does not preclude the fact that the same thread of concern runs throughout her work, or that the stringing of that thread through varying means and materials is as much a part of the nature of her thinking as is any single work or genre.

In fact, it's the protagonist of the title story of her first collection who writes a line in his diary that has since become one of Bachmann's most quoted: "Keine neue Welt ohne neue Sprache" ("No new world without a new language").[17] Not only does this encapsulate what Bachmann was aiming at in all of her writings, it speaks to the many "new worlds" she wished to render in her wide-ranging expression. While it is true that Bachmann simply had more freedom in prose to directly discuss the problems of men and women, history and time, innocence and guilt, etc., it's also true that poetry affords a freer hand with the nuances of speech and metaphor in the search for a "new world" through figurative language. In the end, each dovetails with the other, Bachmann's poems representing the first and most intense crucible of her utopian vision and thought.

First cousin to utopia, however, is disappointment, and there is an increasing sense in Bachmann's later poems that the earlier ideals remain somehow unattainable. Still, in looking at the earliest of her poems that also speak with profound trepidation, one arrives at an appreciation for how Bachmann's late struggle with language and poetry was more with a "type" of expression than with the urge to write itself. For example, the early "Destiny" asks:

> Who knows if we have not already moved
> through many heavens with glazed eyes?
> We, who are banished from time
> and thrust from space,
> we, who are refugees in the night and exiled.

Bachmann's later, uncollected "Exile" would seem a direct extension of "Destiny," yet it approaches its subject from a more grounded perspective, one that acknowledges loss, but also with a greater assurance of what can be retrieved from it. In the last stanzas, the speaker states:

> I with the German language
> this cloud around me
> which I keep as a house
> press through all languages
>
> O how it grows dark
> those muted those rain tones
> only a few fall
>
> Into brighter zones it will lift the dead man up

The "it" being language, here the motions of falling and flight come together and are transformed into a resurrection through words. An exile from her native land (even from the "native" self, given that the speaker is referred to as a "dead *man*" at the beginning of the poem), the writer remains both a prisoner and worshiper of her native tongue. It is all that is left to her, though it as well remains a "cloud." Within it, however, she is able to maintain "a house," just as she can construct a word like "Regentöne" ("rain tones") in order to get at her meaning. Later, in "You Words," Bachmann even goes so far as to address language directly, knowing that

> The word
> will only drag
> other words behind it,
> the sentence a sentence,

but also that her final urge is that "nothing be final/ – not this passion for words,/ nor a saying and its contradiction!"

For Bachmann, the objective is clear, namely "To create a single lasting sentence,/ to persevere in the ding-dong of words" ("Truly"). However, in one of her last poems, "No Delicacies," she refuses to forward the battle through the "delicacies" of traditional poetic speech. Declaring that, "Nothing pleases me anymore," she goes on to examine what she has taken from language, as well as what she cannot redress:

> I have learned an insight
> with words
> that exist
> (for the lowest class)
>
> Hunger
>   Shame

> Tears
>
> and
>
> Darkness.

Knowledge, however, is not enough, nor the determination of her statement that "I despair in the face of despair." Instead, she can only maintain that "I don't neglect writing," refusing "to get by with words" in a watered down fashion. "I am not my assistant," she declares, arguing instead for a defiant act of cancellation at the end of the poem:

> Must I
> with a battered head,
> with the writing cramp in this hand,
> under the pressure of the three hundredth night
> rip up the paper,
> sweep away the scribbled word operas,
> annihilating as well: I you and he she it
>
> we you all?
>
> (Should? The others should.)
>
> My part, it shall be lost.

Though this would seem an ultimate denial of the efficacy of any speech, the conviction behind it is one that still values words. Even in the last poem she completed, "Bohemia Lies by the Sea," a poem she claimed she would always stand by,[18] Bachmann recognizes the border set down and accepts it, if only to maintain hope amid profound doubt, as she writes:

> I still border on a word and on another land,

I border, like little else, on everything more and more,

a Bohemian, a wandering minstrel, who has nothing, who
is held by nothing, gifted only at seeing, by a doubtful sea,
   the land of my choice.

   All of it, however, the struggle and the hope came to a sudden and
tragic end on the night of September 26, 1973, when Bachmann fell
asleep in her apartment in Rome while smoking a cigarette in bed.
She awoke to find herself and the bed engulfed in flames, but by the
time the fire department arrived she was found unconscious and
badly burned. Three weeks later, at the age of forty-seven,
Bachmann was dead, her life and work having met its own "Early
Noon," though writers ranging from Christa Wolf to Uwe Johnson
to Thomas Bernhard would continue to press the limits and wonders
of "The unspeakable...barely spoken" that Bachmann first
explored. Where she herself might have headed, or if she would
indeed return to poetry, is impossible to say, though clearly she
would have soon completed work on the drafts that survive of the
last two novels in her *Todesarten* trilogy. What is clear is that
Bachmann's implicit urge would and does remain to delineate and
step beyond the border of speech first laid down within her poems.
   "To become seeing," writes Hans Höller, "to be able to see, is not
something sought after but also the curse, the deadly consequence
discovered and suffered within the confrontation with historical
experience."[19] That Bachmann was met with this curse and chal-
lenge as a child only a year before W.H. Auden would write in his
elegy to Yeats that "poetry makes nothing happen" illustrates her
courage in facing the reality of her times while examining the very
language used to perceive it. Though ultimately she might agree
with Auden's stoicism, in her flight across the abyss of historical
experience just this side of the border of speech, Bachmann is there
to remind us that the attempt at meaningful speech must still be

made. As she herself writes in "Wozu Gedichte" ("What Good Are Poems"), "The playing field is language, and its borders are the borders of what we gaze on without question, that which is divulged and precisely imagined, experienced in pain, and in happiness celebrated and praised – namely the world."[20] Beyond this, the poet's only responsibility is to endure and embrace what Bachmann expresses best at the end of her "Songs in Flight":

> Love has its triumph and death has one,
> in time and the time beyond us.
> We have none.
>
> Only the sinking of stars. Silence and reflection.
> Yet the song beyond the dust
> will overcome our own.

March 1, 1994

TRANSLATOR'S NOTE

The German text for the poems is from the first volume of *Ingeborg Bachmann, Werke,* eds. Christine Koschel, Inge von Weidenbaum, and Clemens Münster (Munich: Piper, 1978). The only poems of Bachmann that are not translated here are several that are considered to be juvenilia.

Given the simplicity of Bachmann's vocabulary, it is surprising how difficult it can be to render her meaning. However, I have tried to maintain consistency in the imagery and vocabulary that Bachmann uses. I have also tried to remain faithful to meter, stanzaic form, rhyme, and lineation. The rhyme and meter are, of course, the hardest to render, and at times I have had to rely on slant or consonantal rhyme in order not to obscure or violate Bachmann's voice and meaning. However, I have also tried to render those passages in the German where strong rhymes occur in conjunction with alternating weak rhymes.

For the original prodding to read and translate Bachmann's poetry, I am deeply indebted to Joseph Brodsky, as well as to two of my German professors at Columbia University, Howard Stern and Beth Bjorklund, for many insightful conversations about Bachmann and the difficulties of translation. Thanks also go to The Fulbright Commission of Austria for a grant that allowed me to study at the University of Vienna while working on the translations. I am also indebted to two Austrians, Gabriele Kiss and Brigitte Voykowitsch, who read the first drafts. Many thanks also go to Professor Bruce Kieffer of Williams College who read through a partial manuscript at a crucial stage, helping with difficulties in the German, and to Milt Djuric for his advice on how the poems sounded in English.

Finally, the poet's brother, Heinz Bachmann, as well as his wife Sheila, have been extremely kind, helpful, and generous with their time in reading every word of the manuscript and offering countless useful corrections and suggestions. I am also grateful to Bachmann's sister, Isolde Moser, as well as R. Piper Verlag, for granting permission for the these translations, which are dedicated to the brothers Janowski, Krzysztof and Jan, and our time together in Wien.

SONGS IN FLIGHT

Die gestundete Zeit

Borrowed Time

I

Ausfahrt

Vom Lande steigt Rauch auf.
Die kleine Fischerhütte behalt im Aug,
denn die Sonne wird sinken,
ehe du zehn Meilen zurückgelegt hast.

Das dunkle Wasser, tausendäugig,
schlägt die Wimper von weißer Gischt auf,
um dich anzusehen, groß und lang,
dreißig Tage lang.

Auch wenn das Schiff hart stampft
und einen unsicheren Schritt tut,
steh ruhig auf Deck.

An den Tischen essen sie jetzt
den geräucherten Fisch;
dann werden die Männer hinknien
und die Netze flicken,
aber nachts wird geschlafen,
eine Stunde oder zwei Stunden,
und ihre Hände werden weich sein,
frei von Salz und Öl,
weich wie das Brot des Traumes,
von dem sie brechen.

I

Journey Out

Smoke rises from the land.
Remember the tiny fishing huts,
because the sun will sink
before you've set ten miles behind you.

The dark water, thousand-eyed,
opens its white-foamed lashes,
studying you, deep and long,
thirty days long.

Even when the ship pitches hard
and makes each step uncertain,
stand calm on deck.

At the table they eat
the heavily smoked fish;
then the men will kneel
and mend the nets,
though nightly each will sleep
an hour or two,
and their hands will soften,
free from salt and oil,
soft as the bread of the dream
from which they break.

Die erste Welle der Nacht schlägt ans Ufer,
die zweite erreicht schon dich.
Aber wenn du scharf hinüberschaust,
kannst du den Baum noch sehen,
der trotzig den Arm hebt
— einen hat ihm der Wind schon abgeschlagen
— und du denkst: wie lange noch,
wie lange noch
wird das krumme Holz den Wettern standhalten?
Vom Land ist nichts mehr zu sehen.
Du hättest dich mit einer Hand in die Sandbank krallen
oder mit einer Locke an die Klippen heften sollen.

In die Muscheln blasend, gleiten die Ungeheuer des Meers
auf die Rücken der Wellen, sie reiten und schlagen
mit blanken Säbeln die Tage in Stücke, eine rote Spur
bleibt im Wasser, dort legt dich der Schlaf hin,
auf den Rest deiner Stunden,
und dir schwinden die Sinne.

Da ist etwas mit den Tauen geschehen,
man ruft dich, und du bist froh,
daß man dich braucht. Das Beste
ist die Arbeit auf den Schiffen,
die weithin fahren,
das Tauknüpfen, das Wasserschöpfen,
das Wändedichten und das Hüten der Fracht.
Das Beste ist, müde zu sein und am Abend
hinzufallen. Das Beste ist, am Morgen,
mit dem ersten Licht, hell zu werden,
gegen den unverrückbaren Himmel zu stehen,
der ungangbaren Wasser nicht zu achten
und das Schiff über die Wellen zu heben,
auf das immerwiederkehrende Sonnenufer zu.

The first wave of night hits the shore,
the second already reaches you.
But if you stare sharply yonder,
you can still see the tree
which defiantly lifts an arm
– the wind has already knocked one off
– and you think: how much longer,
how much longer
will the twisted timber withstand the weather?
Of land there's nothing more to be seen.
With your hand you should have dug into the sandbank
or tied yourself to the cliff with a strand of hair.

Blowing into conches, sea monsters float
on the crests of waves, they ride and slice
the day to pieces with bright sabers; a red trail
remains in the water, where sleep takes hold of you
for the rest of your hours,
your senses spinning.

But then something happens with the ropes,
you are called and you are happy
that you are needed. Best of all
is the work on ships
that sail far away,
the knotting of ropes, the bailing of water,
the caulking of leaks, the guarding of freight.
Best to be tired and at evening
to collapse. Best in the morning
to awaken clear to the first light,
to rise up beneath the immovable sky,
to ignore the impassable water,
and to lift the ship over the waves
towards the forever recurring shore of the sun.

Abschied von England

Ich habe deinen Boden kaum betreten,
schweigsames Land, kaum einen Stein berührt,
ich war von deinem Himmel so hoch gehoben,
so in Wolken, Dunst und in noch Ferneres gestellt,
daß ich dich schon verließ,
als ich vor Anker ging.

Du hast meine Augen geschlossen
mit Meerhauch und Eichenblatt,
von meinen Tränen begossen,
hieltst du die Gräser satt;
aus meinen Träumen gelöst,
wagten sich Sonnen heran,
doch alles war wieder fort,
wenn dein Tag begann.
Alles blieb ungesagt.

Durch die Straßen flatterten die großen grauen Vögel
und wiesen mich aus.
War ich je hier?

Ich wollte nicht gesehen werden.

Meine Augen sind offen.
Meerhauch und Eichenblatt?
Unter den Schlangen des Meers
seh ich, an deiner Statt,
das Land meiner Seele erliegen.

Ich habe seinen Boden nie betreten.

Departure from England

I have barely stepped upon your land,
silent country, barely disturbed a stone.
I was lifted so high by your sky,
placed so in clouds, mist, and remoteness,
that I had already left you
the moment I set anchor.

You have closed my eyes
with sea breeze and oak leaf,
upon the tears I cried
you let the grasses feed;
out of my dreams, suns dared
to venture across the land,
yet everything disappeared
as soon as your day began.
Everything remained unspoken.

Through streets flapped the great, gray birds
that singled me out for expulsion.
Was I ever here?

I didn't want to be seen.

My eyes are open.
Sea breeze and oak leaf?
Under the serpentine sea
in place of you I see
the country of my soul succumb.

I have never stepped on its land.

Fall ab, Herz

Fall ab, Herz, vom Baum der Zeit,
fallt, ihr Blätter, aus den erkalteten Ästen,
die einst die Sonne umarmt',
fallt, wie Tränen fallen aus dem geweiteten Aug!

Fliegt noch die Locke taglang im Wind
um des Landgotts gebräunte Stirn,
unter dem Hemd preßt die Faust
schon die klaffende Wunde.

Drum sei hart, wenn der zarte Rücken der Wolken
sich dir einmal noch beugt,
nimm es für nichts, wenn der Hymettos die Waben
noch einmal dir füllt.

Denn wenig gilt dem Landmann ein Halm in der Dürre,
wenig ein Sommer vor unserem großen Geschlecht.

Und was bezeugt schon dein Herz?
Zwischen gestern und morgen schwingt es,
lautlos und fremd,
und was es schlägt,
ist schon sein Fall aus der Zeit.

Fall Down, Heart

Fall down, heart, from the tree of time,
fall, you leaves, from icy branches
that once the sun embraced,
fall, as tears fall from longing eyes.

Though his curls whip for days in the wind
around the land god's umber brow,
under the shirt a fist presses
already to the gaping wound.

Be hard, if the tender backs of clouds
bend yet again to you;
take it as nothing, if Hymettus's honeycombs
once more fill you up.

Because one stalk in a drought means little to farmers,
one summer so little to our great lineage.

And so what can your heart attest to?
Between yesterday and tomorrow it swings,
soundless and strange,
and what it beats
is its own fall out of time.

Dunkles zu sagen

Wie Orpheus spiel ich
auf den Saiten des Lebens den Tod
und in die Schönheit der Erde
und deiner Augen, die den Himmel verwalten,
weiß ich nur Dunkles zu sagen.

Vergiß nicht, daß auch du, plötzlich,
an jenem Morgen, als dein Lager
noch naß war von Tau und die Nelke
an deinem Herzen schlief,
den dunklen Fluß sahst,
der an dir vorbeizog.

Die Saite des Schweigens
gespannt auf die Welle von Blut,
griff ich dein tönendes Herz.
Verwandelt ward deine Locke
ins Schattenhaar der Nacht,
der Finsternis schwarze Flocken
beschneiten dein Antlitz.

Und ich gehör dir nicht zu.
Beide klagen wir nun.

Aber wie Orpheus weiß ich
auf der Seite des Todes das Leben,
und mir blaut
dein für immer geschlossenes Aug.

Darkness Spoken

Like Orpheus I play
death on the strings of life,
and to the beauty of the Earth
and your eyes, which govern heaven,
I can only speak of darkness.

Don't forget that you also, suddenly,
on that morning when your camp
was still damp with dew, and a carnation
slept on your heart,
you saw the dark stream
race past you.

The string of silence
taut on the pulse of blood,
I grasped your beating heart.
Your curls were transformed
into the shadow hair of night,
black flakes of darkness
buried your face.

And I don't belong to you.
Both of us mourn now.

But like Orpheus I know
life on the strings of death,
deepening the blue
of your forever closed eye.

Paris

Aufs Rad der Nacht geflochten
schlafen die Verlorenen
in den donnernden Gängen unten,
doch wo wir sind, ist Licht.

Wir haben die Arme voll Blumen,
Mimosen aus vielen Jahren;
Goldnes fällt von Brücke zu Brücke
atemlos in den Fluß.

Kalt ist das Licht,
noch kälter der Stein vor dem Tor,
und die Schalen der Brunnen
sind schon zur Hälfte geleert.

Was wird sein, wenn wir, vom Heimweh
benommen bis ans fliehende Haar,
hier bleiben und fragen: was wird sein,
wenn wir die Schönheit bestehen?

Auf den Wagen des Lichts gehoben,
wachend auch, sind wir verloren,
auf den Straßen der Genien oben,
doch wo wir nicht sind, ist Nacht.

Paris

Lashed to the wheel of night
the lost ones sleep
in the thunderous passages beneath;
but where we are, is light.

Our arms are full of blossoms,
mimosa from many years;
goldness showers from bridge after bridge
breathless into the stream.

Cold is the light,
still colder the stone before the gate,
and the basins of fountains
are already half empty.

What will happen if we, homesick
and helpless with windblown hair,
remain here and ask: what will happen
if we survive the test of beauty?

Lifted onto the wagon of light,
and waking, we are lost
in the alleys of brilliance above;
but where we are not, is night.

Die große Fracht

Die große Fracht des Sommers ist verladen,
das Sonnenschiff im Hafen liegt bereit,
wenn hinter dir die Möwe stürzt und schreit.
Die große Fracht des Sommers ist verladen.

Das Sonnenschiff im Hafen liegt bereit,
und auf die Lippen der Galionsfiguren
tritt unverhüllt das Lächeln der Lemuren.
Das Sonnenschiff im Hafen liegt bereit.

Wenn hinter dir die Möwe stürzt und schreit,
kommt aus dem Westen der Befehl zu sinken;
doch offnen Augs wirst du im Licht ertrinken,
wenn hinter dir die Möwe stürzt und schreit.

The Heavy Cargo

The summer's heavy cargo has been loaded,
waiting in the harbor a sun ship lies,
as at your back the sea gull dips and cries.
The summer's heavy cargo has been loaded.

Waiting in the harbor a sun ship lies,
and there upon the lips of figureheads
the lemur's mocking smile appears and spreads.
Waiting in the harbor a sun ship lies.

As at your back the sea gull dips and cries,
from the western horizon comes the order to sink;
you'll drown, open-eyed, in the light you'll drink,
as at your back the sea gull dips and cries.

Reigen

Reigen – die Liebe hält manchmal
im Löschen der Augen ein,
und wir sehen in ihre eignen
erloschenen Augen hinein.

Kalter Rauch aus dem Krater
haucht unsre Wimpern an;
es hielt die schreckliche Leere
nur einmal den Atem an.

Wir haben die toten Augen
gesehn und vergessen nie.
Die Liebe währt am längsten
und sie erkennt uns nie.

Reigen

Reigen – a love can sometimes cease
in the extinguishing of an eye,
and what we come to see
is love's extinguished eye.

Cold smoke from the crater
breathes upon on our lashes;
only once did empty terror
not breathe at all upon us.

We've seen the eyes of the dead
and will forget them never.
Love lasts to the end,
but apprehends us never.

Herbstmanöver

Ich sage nicht: das war gestern. Mit wertlosem
Sommergeld in den Taschen liegen wir wieder
auf der Spreu des Hohns, im Herbstmanöver der Zeit.
Und der Fluchtweg nach Süden kommt uns nicht,
wie den Vögeln, zustatten. Vorüber, am Abend,
ziehen Fischkutter und Gondeln, und manchmal
trifft mich ein Splitter traumsatten Marmors,
wo ich verwundbar bin, durch Schönheit, im Aug.

In den Zeitungen lese ich viel von der Kälte
und ihren Folgen, von Törichten und Toten,
von Vertriebenen, Mördern und Myriaden
von Eisschollen, aber wenig, was mir behagt.
Warum auch? Vor dem Bettler, der mittags kommt,
schlag ich die Tür zu, denn es ist Frieden
und man kann sich den Anblick ersparen, aber nicht
im Regen das freudlose Sterben der Blätter.

Laßt uns eine Reise tun! Laßt uns unter Zypressen
oder auch unter Palmen oder in den Orangenhainen
zu verbilligten Preisen Sonnenuntergänge sehen,
die nicht ihresgleichen haben! Laßt uns die
unbeantworteten Briefe an das Gestern vergessen!
Die Zeit tut Wunder. Kommt sie uns aber unrecht,
mit dem Pochen der Schuld: wir sind nicht zu Hause.
Im Keller des Herzens, schlaflos, find ich mich wieder
auf der Spreu des Hohns, im Herbstmanöver der Zeit.

Autumn Maneuver

I don't say: ah, yesterday. With worthless
summer money pocketed, we lie again
on the chaff of scorn, in time's autumn maneuver.
And the escape southward isn't feasible for us
as it is for the birds. In the evening
trawlers and gondolas pass, and sometimes
a splinter of dream-filled marble pierces me
in the eye, where I am most vulnerable to beauty.

In the papers I read about the cold
and its effects, about fools and dead men,
about exiles, murderers and myriads
of ice floes, but little that comforts me.
Why should it be otherwise? In the face of the beggar
who comes at noon I slam the door, for we live in peacetime
and one can spare oneself such a sight, but not
the joyless dying of leaves in the rain.

Let's take a trip! Let us stroll under cypresses
or even under palms or in the orange groves
to see at reduced rates sunsets
that are beyond compare! Let us forget
the unanswered letters to yesterday!
Time works wonders. But if it arrives inconveniently
with the knocking of guilt: we're not at home.
In the heart's cellar, sleepless, I find myself again
on the chaff of scorn, in time's autumn maneuver.

Die gestundete Zeit

Es kommen härtere Tage.
Die auf Widerruf gestundete Zeit
wird sichtbar am Horizont.
Bald mußt du den Schuh schnüren
und die Hunde zurückjagen in die Marschhöfe.
Denn die Eingeweide der Fische
sind kalt geworden im Wind.
Ärmlich brennt das Licht der Lupinen.
Dein Blick spurt im Nebel:
die auf Widerruf gestundete Zeit
wird sichtbar am Horizont.

Drüben versinkt dir die Geliebte im Sand,
er steigt um ihr wehendes Haar,
er fällt ihr ins Wort,
er befiehlt ihr zu schweigen,
er findet sie sterblich
und willig dem Abschied
nach jeder Umarmung.

Sieh dich nicht um.
Schnür deinen Schuh.
Jag die Hunde zurück.
Wirf die Fische ins Meer.
Lösch die Lupinen!

Es kommen härtere Tage.

Borrowed Time

Harder days are coming.
The loan of borrowed time
will be due on the horizon.
Soon you must lace up your boots
and chase the hounds back to the marsh farms.
For the entrails of fish
have grown cold in the wind.
Dimly burns the light of lupines.
Your gaze makes out in fog:
the loan of borrowed time
will be due on the horizon.

There your loved one sinks in sand;
it rises up to her windblown hair,
it cuts her short,
it commands her to be silent,
it discovers she's mortal
and willing to leave you
after every embrace.

Don't look around.
Lace up your boots.
Chase back the hounds.
Throw the fish into the sea.
Put out the lupines!

Harder days are coming.

II

Sterne im März

Noch ist die Aussaat weit. Auf treten
Vorfelder im Regen und Sterne im März.
In die Formel unfruchtbarer Gedanken
fügt sich das Universum nach dem Beispiel
des Lichts, das nicht an den Schnee rührt.

Unter dem Schnee wird auch Staub sein
und, was nicht zerfiel, des Staubes
spätere Nahrung. O Wind, der anhebt!
Wieder reißen Pflüge das Dunkel auf.
Die Tage wollen länger werden.

An langen Tagen sät man uns ungefragt
in jene krummen und geraden Linien,
und Sterne treten ab. Auf den Feldern
gedeihen oder verderben wir wahllos,
gefügig dem Regen und zuletzt auch dem Licht.

II

March Stars

Still it's too early for sowing. Fields
surface in rain, March stars appear.
Like an afterthought, the universe submits
to familiar equations, such as the light
that falls but leaves the snow untouched.

Under the snow there will also be dust
and, what doesn't disintegrate, the dust's
later nourishment. O wind, picking up.
Again the plows rip open the darkness.
Each new day will want to be longer.

It's on long days that we are sown,
unasked, in those neat and crooked rows,
as stars sink away above. In fields
we thrive or rot without a choice,
submitting to rain and also at last the light.

Im Zwielicht

Wieder legen wir beide die Hände ins Feuer,
du für den Wein der lange gelagerten Nacht,
ich für den Morgenquell, der die Kelter nicht kennt.
Es harrt der Blasbalg des Meisters, dem wir vertrauen.

Wie die Sorge ihn wärmt, tritt der Bläser hinzu.
Er geht, eh es tagt, er kommt, eh du rufst, er ist alt
wie das Zwielicht auf unsren schütteren Brauen.

Wieder kocht er das Blei im Kessel der Tränen,
dir für ein Glas – es gilt, das Versäumte zu feiern –
mir für den Scherben voll Rauch – der wird überm Feuer
     geleert.
So stoß ich zu dir und bringe die Schatten zum Klingen.

Erkannt ist, wer jetzt zögert,
erkannt, wer den Spruch vergaß.
Du kannst und willst ihn nicht wissen,
du trinkst vom Rand, wo es kühl ist
und wie vorzeiten, du trinkst und bleibst nüchtern,
dir wachsen noch Brauen, dir sieht man noch zu!

Ich aber bin schon des Augenblicks
gewärtig in Liebe, mir fällt der Scherben
ins Feuer, mir wird er zum Blei,
das er war. Und hinter der Kugel
steh ich, einäugig, zielsicher, schmal,
und schick sie dem Morgen entgegen.

In Twilight

Again we both swear to what we each hold as true,
you reaching for the wine of the seasoned night,
I for morning's wellspring that knows no winery.
The bellows await the master in whom we trust.

As sorrow warms him, the glassblower steps toward us.
He leaves before dawn, he comes before you call,
he's as old as the twilight on our thin brows.

Again he boils the lead in the kettle of tears,
for you a glass – meaning a toast to the unattained –
for me a shard full of smoke – it's emptied over the fire. And
so I lean towards you, making the shadows ring.

Known now is he who hesitates,
known now is he who forgot the pithy saying.
You can't and don't want to know it,
you drink from the rim where it's cool;
and like long ago, you drink and stay sober,
your brows are still growing, you are still admired!

But I am already prepared
for the moment of love, as the shards fall
into the fire, where they return to the lead
they once were. And behind the bullet
I stand, one-eyed, with a steady aim, slender,
and shoot it towards the morning.

Holz und Späne

Von den Hornissen will ich schweigen,
denn sie sind leicht zu erkennen.
Auch die laufenden Revolutionen
sind nicht gefährlich.
Der Tod im Gefolge des Lärms
ist beschlossen von jeher.

Doch vor den Eintagsfliegen und den Frauen
nimm dich in acht, vor den Sonntagsjägern,
den Kosmetikern, den Unentschiedenen, Wohlmeinenden,
von keiner Verachtung getroffnen.

Aus den Wäldern trugen wir Reisig und Stämme,
und die Sonne ging uns lange nicht auf.
Berauscht vom Papier am Fließband,
erkenn ich die Zweige nicht wieder,
noch das Moos, in dunkleren Tinten gegoren,
noch das Wort, in die Rinden geschnitten,
wahr und vermessen.

Blätterverschleiß, Spruchbänder,
schwarze Plakate . . . Bei Tag und bei Nacht
bebt, unter diesen und jenen Sternen,
die Maschine des Glaubens. Aber ins Holz,
solang es noch grün ist, und mit der Galle,
solang sie noch bitter ist, bin ich
zu schreiben gewillt, was im Anfang war!

Seht zu, daß ihr wachbleibt!

Wood and Shavings

Of hornets I will say nothing,
since they are so easy to spot.
Also, the current revolutions
are not that dangerous.
Death has always been resolved
in the fanfare of noise.

Yet beware the May flies and women,
beware the Sunday hunters,
beauticians, the undecided, the well meaning,
the ones devoid of contempt.

Out of the forests we carried branches and logs,
and for a long time there was no sun.
Intoxicated by paper on the conveyer belt,
I no longer recognize the branches
or the moss, dyed in darker tints,
or the word, carved into the bark,
impudent and true.

Wasted paper, banners,
black posters… By day and by night
the machine of faith rumbles beneath
this or that star. But in wood,
as long as it is still green, and with gall,
as long as it is still bitter, I am
willing to write what happened at the start!

Make sure you stay awake.

Der Spur der Späne, die flogen, folgt
der Hornissenschwarm, und am Brunnen
sträubt sich der Lockung,
die uns einst schwächte,
das Haar.

The swarm of hornets chases the shavings
blown by the wind, while at the fountain,
resisting the curled allure
that once made us weak,
my hair bristles.

Thema und Variation

In diesem Sommer blieb der Honig aus.
Die Königinnen zogen Schwärme fort,
der Erdbeerschlag war über Tag verdorrt,
die Beerensammler kehrten früh nach Haus.

Die ganze Süße trug ein Strahl des Lichts
in einen Schlaf. Wer schlief ihn vor der Zeit?
Honig und Beeren? Der ist ohne Leid,
dem alles zukommt. Und es fehlt ihm nichts.

Und es fehlt ihm nichts, nur ein wenig,
um zu ruhen oder um aufrecht zu stehen.
Höhlen beugten ihn tief und Schatten,
denn kein Land nahm ihn auf.
Selbst in den Bergen war er nicht sicher
– ein Partisan, den die Welt abgab
an ihren toten Trabanten, den Mond.

Der ist ohne Leid, dem alles zukommt,
und was kam ihm nicht zu? Die Kohorte
der Käfer schlug sich in seiner Hand, Brände
häuften Narben in seinem Gesicht und die Quelle
trat als Chimäre vor sein Aug,
wo sie nicht war.

Honig und Beeren?
Hätte er je den Geruch gekannt, er wär ihm längst
   gefolgt!

Theme and Variation

All summer long the hives produced no honey.
Queen bees gave up and led their swarms away,
strawberries withered, dried up in a day,
and without work, the gatherers went home early.

All tenderness was carried on a beam of light,
a single night's sleep. Who slept before this happened?
Honey and berries? He knows no misfortune,
he who lacks for nothing. For him, it all comes right.

And he lacks for nothing, except just a little,
when wanting to rest or stand completely erect.
For he's bent double by caves and shadows
because no country gave him asylum.
Even in the mountains he didn't feel safe
– a partisan, whom the world had turned away
to its own dead satellite, the moon.

He knows no misfortune, he who lacks for nothing,
and what did he ever lack? The beetle's
brethren drank from his hand, firebrands
etched stigmata upon his face, and the wellspring
appeared as a chimera before his eyes
where it was not.

Honey and berries?
Had he known their scent, he would've followed it long ago.

Nachtwandlerischer Schlaf im Gehen,
wer schlief ihn vor der Zeit?
Einer, der alt geboren wurde
und früh ins Dunkel muß.
Die ganze Süße trug ein Strahl des Lichts
an ihm vorbei.

Er spie ins Unterholz den Fluch,
der Dürre bringt, er schrie
und ward erhört:
die Beerensammler kehrten früh nach Haus!
Als sich die Wurzel hob
und ihnen pfeifend nachglitt,
blieb eine Schlangenhaut des Baumes letzte Hut.
Der Erdbeerschlag war über Tag verdorrt.

Unten im Dorf standen die Eimer leer
und trommelreif im Hof.
So schlug die Sonne zu
und wirbelte den Tod.

Die Fenster fielen zu,
die Königinnen zogen Schwärme fort,
und keiner hinderte sie, fortzufliegen.
Die Wildnis nahm sie auf,
der hohle Baum im Farn
den ersten freien Staat.
Den letzten Menschen traf
ein Stachel ohne Schmerz.

In diesem Sommer blieb der Honig aus.

Walking through sleep, sleepwalking,
who slept before this happened?
One who was born elderly
and is called to darkness early.
All tenderness was carried on a beam of light
eluding him.

He spat a curse into the undergrowth
that brought on drought, for in screaming
he was heard:
without work, the gatherers went home early!
When the root lifted itself
and, hissing, slithered away,
a snakeskin remained, the tree's defense.
Strawberries withered, dried up in a day.

In the village below the bucket stood empty,
ready to be used as a drum in the square.
Already the sun had struck
and spun around death.

The windows slammed shut,
queen bees gave up and led their swarms away,
and no one stopped them from flying off.
The wilderness accepted them,
their hollow tree among ferns
the first free state.
The very last person, pricked
by a thorn, could feel no pain.

All summer long the hives produced no honey.

Früher Mittag

Still grünt die Linde im eröffneten Sommer,
weit aus den Städten gerückt, flirrt
der mattglänzende Tagmond. Schon ist Mittag,
schon regt sich im Brunnen der Strahl,
schon hebt sich unter den Scherben
des Märchenvogels geschundener Flügel,
und die vom Steinwurf entstellte Hand
sinkt ins erwachende Korn.

Wo Deutschlands Himmel die Erde schwärzt,
sucht sein enthaupteter Engel ein Grab für den Haß
und reicht dir die Schüssel des Herzens.

Eine Handvoll Schmerz verliert sich über den Hügel.

Sieben Jahre später
fällt es dir wieder ein,
am Brunnen vor dem Tore,
blick nicht zu tief hinein,
die Augen gehen dir über.

Sieben Jahre später,
in einem Totenhaus,
trinken die Henker von gestern
den goldenen Becher aus.
Die Augen täten dir sinken.

Early Noon

Silently the linden greens in approaching summer,
far from the cities there glimmers
the pale brightness of the day moon. Already it's noon,
already a sunbeam flashes in the fountain,
already the fabulous bird's flayed wing
lifts itself beneath the rubble,
and the hand that's cramped from casting stones
sinks into the budding corn.

Where Germany's sky blackens the earth,
its beheaded angel seeks a grave for hate
and offers you the bowl of the heart.

A handful of pain vanishes over the hill.

Seven years later
it occurs to you again,
at the fountain before the portal,
don't look too deep within,
as your eyes fill with tears.

Seven years later,
inside a mortuary,
the hangmen of yesterday
drain the golden cup.
Your eyes lower in shame.

Schon ist Mittag, in der Asche
krümmt sich das Eisen, auf den Dorn
ist die Fahne gehißt, und auf den Felsen
uralten Traums bleibt fortan
der Adler geschmiedet.

Nur die Hoffnung kauert erblindet im Licht.

Lös ihr die Fessel, führ sie
die Halde herab, leg ihr
die Hand auf das Aug, daß sie
kein Schatten versengt!

Wo Deutschlands Erde den Himmel schwärzt,
sucht die Wolke nach Worten und füllt den Krater mit
    Schweigen,
eh sie der Sommer im schütteren Regen vernimmt.

Das Unsägliche geht, leise gesagt, übers Land:
schon ist Mittag.

Already it's noon, in embers
the iron bends, on the thorn
the flag is hoisted, and onto the cliff
of the ancient dream the eagle is welded,
remaining forever.

Only hope cowers, blinded in the light.

Throw off its shackles, help it
down the slope, cover
its eyes so that
the shadows don't scorch it!

Where Germany's earth blackens the sky,
a cloud seeks words and fills the crater with silence
before summer is made aware of its sparse rain.

The unspeakable passes, barely spoken, over the land:
already it's noon.

Alle Tage

Der Krieg wird nicht mehr erklärt,
sondern fortgesetzt. Das Unerhörte
ist alltäglich geworden. Der Held
bleibt den Kämpfen fern. Der Schwache
ist in die Feuerzonen gerückt.
Die Uniform des Tages ist die Geduld,
die Auszeichnung der armselige Stern
der Hoffnung über dem Herzen.

Er wird verliehen,
wenn nichts mehr geschieht,
wenn das Trommelfeuer verstummt,
wenn der Feind unsichtbar geworden ist
und der Schatten ewiger Rüstung
den Himmel bedeckt.

Er wird verliehen
für die Flucht von den Fahnen,
für die Tapferkeit vor dem Freund,
für den Verrat unwürdiger Geheimnisse
und die Nichtachtung
jeglichen Befehls.

Every Day

War is no longer declared,
but rather continued. The outrageous
has become the everyday. The hero
is absent from the battle. The weak
are moved into the firing zone.
The uniform of the day is patience,
the order of merit is the wretched star
of hope over the heart.

It is awarded
when nothing more happens,
when the bombardment is silenced,
when the enemy has become invisible
and the shadow of eternal weapons
covers the sky.

It is awarded
for deserting the flag,
for bravery before a friend,
for the betrayal of shameful secrets
and the disregard
of every command.

Einem Feldherrn

Wenn jenes Geschäft im Namen der Ehre
ergrauter und erblindeter Völker
wieder zustande kommt, wirst du
ein Handlanger sein und dienstbar
unsren Gemarkungen, da du's verstehst,
sie einzufrieden mit Blut.
Voraus in den Büchern schattet
dein Name, und es verleitet
sein Anflug den Lorbeer zum Wuchs.

Wie wir's verstehen: opfre keinem vor dir
und rufe auch Gott nicht an. (Verlangte ihn je
teilzuhaben an deiner Beute? War er je
ein Parteigänger deiner Hoffnungen?)

Eins sollst du wissen:
erst wenn du nicht mehr versuchst,
wie viele vor dir, mit dem Degen
den unteilbaren Himmel zu trennen,
treibt der Lorbeer ein Blatt.
Erst wenn du mit einem ungeheuren Zweifel
dein Glück aus dem Sattel hebst und selbst
aufspringst, verheiß ich dir Sieg!

Denn du errangst ihn nicht damals,
als dein Glück für dich siegte;
zwar sanken die Fahnen des Feindes
und Waffen fielen dir zu
und Früchte aus Gärten,
die ein andrer bebaute.

To a General

When that affair in the name of the honor
of blind and gray-haired nations
again comes to pass, you will be
the drudge tending to our boundaries,
because you know
how to fence them in with blood.
Already your name shadows
the books, its presence seducing
a sprig of laurel into growth.

To us, it is so: don't make sacrifices to anyone
and don't invoke God. (Did he ever
demand a cut of your spoils? Was he ever
a party to your hopes?)

There's one thing you should know:
only then, when you no longer attempt,
as many before you, to part
the unseverable sky with the sword
will the laurel sprout a leaf.
Only when, with monstrous doubt,
you lift your luck out of the saddle
and step down yourself, will I promise you victory!

For you won no victory then
when your luck won it for you;
indeed, the enemy's flags sank
and weapons fell to you
and fruit from the gardens,
which another tended.

Wo am Horizont der Weg deines Glücks
und der Weg deines Unglücks
in eins verlaufen, richte die Schlacht.
Wo es dunkelt und die Soldaten schlafen,
wo sie dir fluchten und von dir
verflucht wurden, richte den Tod.

Du wirst fallen
vom Berg ins Tal, mit den reißenden Gewässern
in die Schluchten, auf den Grund der Fruchtbarkeit,
in die Samen der Erde, dann in die Minen von Gold,
in den Fluß des Erzes, aus dem die Standbilder
der Großen gehämmert werden, in die tiefen Bezirke
des Vergessens, Millionen Klafter von dort,
und in die Bergwerke des Traums.
Zuletzt aber in das Feuer.

Dort reicht dir der Lorbeer ein Blatt.

Where, on the horizon, the path of your luck
and the path of your bad luck
converge, prepare for battle.
Where darkness falls and the troops sleep,
where they will curse you and by you
are cursed, prepare for death.

You will fall
from the mountain into the valley, with rapids
into the ravine, into fecund soil,
into the seeds of the earth, then into the gold mines,
into the river of ore from which the statues
of the great are hammered, into the deep realm
of forgetfulness, a million fathoms farther
and into the pit of the dream.
Then finally into the fire.

There the laurel will offer you a leaf.

Botschaft

Aus der leichenwarmen Vorhalle des Himmels tritt die Sonne.
Es sind dort nicht die Unsterblichen,
sondern die Gefallenen, vernehmen wir.

Und Glanz kehrt sich nicht an Verwesung. Unsere Gottheit,
die Geschichte, hat uns ein Grab bestellt,
aus dem es keine Auferstehung gibt.

Message

Out of the corpse-warm foyer of the sky steps the sun.
There it is not the immortals,
but rather the fallen, we perceive.

And brilliance doesn't trouble itself with decay.
Our Godhead, History, has ordered for us a grave
from which there is no resurrection.

III

Die Brücken

Straffer zieht der Wind das Band vor den Brücken.

An den Traversen zerrieb
der Himmel sein dunkelstes Blau.
Hüben und drüben wechseln
im Licht unsre Schatten.

Pont Mirabeau . . . Waterloobridge . . .
Wie ertragen's die Namen,
die Namenlosen zu tragen?

Von den Verlornen gerührt,
die der Glaube nicht trug,
erwachen die Trommeln im Fluß.

Einsam sind alle Brücken,
und der Ruhm ist ihnen gefährlich
wie uns, vermeinen wir doch,
die Schritte der Sterne
auf unserer Schulter zu spüren.
Doch übers Gefälle des Vergänglichen
wölbt uns kein Traum.

III

The Bridges

Wind tightens the ribbon drawn across bridges.

The sky grinds on the crossbeams
with its darkest blue.
On this side and that our shadows
pass each the other in the light.

Pont Mirabeau... Waterloo Bridge...
How can the names stand
to carry the nameless?

Stirred by the lost
that faith could not carry,
the river's drumbeat awakens.

Lonely are all bridges,
and fame is as dangerous for them
as it is for us, yet we presume
to feel the tread of stars
upon our shoulders.
Still, over the slope of transience
no dream arches us.

Besser ist's, im Auftrag der Ufer
zu leben, von einem zum andern,
und tagsüber zu wachen,
daß das Band der Berufene trennt.
Denn er erreicht die Schere der Sonne
im Nebel, und wenn sie ihn blendet,
umfängt ihn der Nebel im Fall.

It's better to follow the riverbanks,
crossing from one to another,
and all day keep an eye out
for the official to cut the ribbon.
For when he does, he'll seize the sun's scissors
within the fog, and if the sun blinds him,
he'll be swallowed by fog when he falls.

Nachtflug

Unser Acker ist der Himmel,
im Schweiß der Motoren bestellt,
angesichts der Nacht,
unter Einsatz des Traums –

geträumt auf Schädelstätten und Scheiterhaufen,
unter dem Dach der Welt, dessen Ziegel
der Wind forttrug – und nun Regen, Regen, Regen
in unserem Haus und in den Mühlen
die blinden Flüge der Fledermäuse.
Wer wohnte dort? Wessen Hände waren rein?
Wer leuchtete in der Nacht,
Gespenst den Gespenstern?

Im Stahlgefieder geborgen, verhören
Instrumente den Raum, Kontrolluhren und Skalen
das Wolkengesträuch, und es streift die Liebe
unsres Herzens vergessene Sprache:
kurz und lang lang . . . Für eine Stunde
rührt Hagel die Trommel des Ohrs,
das, uns abgeneigt, lauscht und verwindet.

Nicht untergegangen sind Sonne und Erde,
nur als Gestirne gewandert und nicht zu erkennen.

Wir sind aufgestiegen von einem Hafen,
wo Wiederkehr nicht zählt
und nicht Fracht und nicht Fang.
Indiens Gewürze und Seiden aus Japan
gehören den Händlern
wie die Fische den Netzen.

Night Flight

Our land is the sky
sown with the engine's sweat,
in the face of night,
before the ascent of dreams —

dreamt on Calvary and on funeral pyres,
under the roof of the world, whose shingles
the wind carried off — and now rain, rain, rain
in our house, and in the mills
the blind flight of the bats.
Who lived there? Whose hands were pure?
Who shone in the night,
a ghost to other ghosts?

Protected by steel feathers, instruments
sound out space, control clocks and dials
probe thickets of clouds, and love touches
the forgotten speech of our heart:
short and long long… For an hour
hail taps the drum of the ear
that, reluctantly, listens in and endures.

Sun and earth have not sunk,
they only wander as stars, unrecognizable.

We have taken off from a port
where the return doesn't matter,
nor the cargo, nor the haul.
Indian spices and silks from Japan
belong to the dealers
like fish to the nets.

Doch ein Geruch ist zu spüren,
vorlaufend den Kometen,
und das Gewebe der Luft,
von gefallnen Kometen zerrissen.
Nenn's den Status der Einsamen,
in dem sich das Staunen vollzieht.
Nichts weiter.

Wir sind aufgestiegen, und die Klöster sind leer,
seit wir dulden, ein Orden, der nicht heilt und nicht lehrt.
Zu handeln ist nicht Sache der Piloten. Sie haben
Stützpunkte im Aug und auf den Knien ausgebreitet
die Landkarte einer Welt, der nichts hinzuzufügen ist.

Wer lebt dort unten? Wer weint . . .
Wer verliert den Schlüssel zum Haus?
Wer findet sein Bett nicht, wer schläft
auf den Schwellen? Wer, wenn der Morgen kommt,
wagt's, den Silberstreifen zu deuten: seht, über mir . . .
Wenn das Wasser von neuem ins Mühlrad greift,
wer wagt's, sich der Nacht zu erinnern?

Yet a fragrance can be traced
preceding the comets
and the air's fabric
ripped by those fallen.
Call it the status of the lonely
in whom wonder still occurs.
Nothing more.

We've taken off, and the cloisters are empty,
since we endure, an order that can't heal or teach.
It's not the pilots' job to act. They have
the air bases in sight, and spread out on their knees
the map of a world, to which nothing can be added.

Who lives below? Who is crying…
Who has lost the key to his house?
Who can't find his bed, who sleeps
on the doorstep? Who, when morning comes,
dares to interpret the silver bands: look, above me…
When water churns the mill wheel again,
who will dare to remember the night?

Psalm

1

Schweigt mit mir, wie alle Glocken schweigen!

In der Nachgeburt der Schrecken
sucht das Geschmeiß nach neuer Nahrung.
Zur Ansicht hängt karfreitags eine Hand
am Firmament, zwei Finger fehlen ihr,
sie kann nicht schwören, daß alles,
alles nicht gewesen sei und nichts
sein wird. Sie taucht ins Wolkenrot,
entrückt die neuen Mörder
und geht frei.

Nachts auf dieser Erde
in Fenster greifen, die Linnen zurückschlagen,
daß der Kranken Heimlichkeit bloßliegt,
ein Geschwür voll Nahrung, unendliche Schmerzen
für jeden Geschmack.

Die Metzger halten, behandschuht,
den Atem der Entblößten an,
der Mond in der Tür fällt zu Boden,
laß die Scherben liegen, den Henkel . . .

Alles war gerichtet für die letzte Ölung.
(Das Sakrament kann nicht vollzogen werden.)

Psalm

I

Be silent with me, as all bells are silent!

Amid the afterbirth of terror
the rabble grovels for new nourishment.
On Good Friday a hand hangs on display
in the firmament, two fingers missing,
and it cannot swear that all of it,
all of it didn't happen, nor that
it ever will. It dives into red clouds,
whisks off the new murderers
and goes free.

Each night on this earth
open the windows, fold back the sheets
so that the invalid's secret lies naked,
a sore full of sustenance, endless pain
for every taste.

Gloved butchers cease
the breath of the naked;
the moon in the doorway falls to earth;
let the pieces lie, the handle…

All was prepared for the last rites.
(The sacrament cannot be completed.)

2

Wie eitel alles ist.
Wälze eine Stadt heran,
erhebe dich aus dem Staub dieser Stadt,
übernimm ein Amt
und verstelle dich,
um der Bloßstellung zu entgehen.

Löse die Versprechen ein
vor einem blinden Spiegel in der Luft,
vor einer verschlossenen Tür im Wind.

Unbegangen sind die Wege auf der Steilwand des Himmels.

3

O Augen, an dem Sonnenspeicher Erde verbrannt,
mit der Regenlast aller Augen beladen,
und jetzt versponnen, verwebt
von den tragischen Spinnen
der Gegenwart . . .

4

In die Mulde meiner Stummheit
leg ein Wort
und zieh Wälder groß zu beiden Seiten,
daß mein Mund
ganz im Schatten liegt.

2

How vain it all is.
Roll into a city,
rise from the city's dust,
take over a post
and disguise yourself
to avoid exposure.

Fulfill the promises
before a tarnished mirror in the air,
before a shut door in the wind.

Untraveled are the paths on the steep slope of heaven.

3

O eyes, scorched by the reservoir of sun on earth,
weighted with the rain of all eyes,
and now absorbed, interwoven
by the tragic spiders
of the present...

4

In the hollow of my muteness
lay a word
and raise tall forests on both sides,
such that my mouth
lies wholly in shade.

Im Gewitter der Rosen

Wohin wir uns wenden im Gewitter der Rosen,
ist die Nacht von Dornen erhellt, und der Donner
des Laubs, das so leise war in den Büschen,
folgt uns jetzt auf dem Fuß.

In the Storm of Roses

Wherever we turn in the storm of roses,
the night is lit up by thorns, and the thunder
of leaves, once so quiet within the bushes,
rumbling at our heels.

Salz und Brot

Nun schickt der Wind die Schienen voraus,
wir werden folgen in langsamen Zügen
und diese Inseln bewohnen,
Vertrauen gegen Vertrauen.

In die Hand meines ältesten Freunds leg ich
mein Amt zurück; es verwaltet der Regenmann
jetzt mein finsteres Haus und ergänzt
im Schuldbuch die Linien, die ich zog,
seit ich seltener blieb.

Du, im fieberweißen Ornat,
holst die Verbannten ein und reißt
aus dem Fleisch der Kakteen einen Stachel
– das Zeichen der Ohnmacht,
dem wir uns willenlos beugen.

Wir wissen,
daß wir des Kontinentes Gefangene bleiben
und seinen Kränkungen wieder verfallen,
und die Gezeiten der Wahrheit
werden nicht seltener sein.

Schläft doch im Felsen
der wenig erleuchtete Schädel,
die Kralle hängt in der Kralle
im dunklen Gestein, und verheilt
sind die Stigmen am Violett des Vulkans.

Von den großen Gewittern des Lichts
hat keines die Leben erreicht.

Salt and Bread

Now the wind sends its rails ahead;
we will follow in slow trains
and inhabit these islands,
intimacy exchanged for intimacy.

Into the hand of my oldest friend
I place the key to my post; the rain man will now manage
my darkened house and complete
the lines of the ledger which I drew up
after I was seldom around.

You, in fever-white vestments,
gather the exiled and tear,
from the flesh of cactus, a thorn
— symbol of impotence
to which we meakly bow.

We know
that we'll remain the continent's captives,
and again we'll succumb to its troubled ills,
and the tides of truth
will be no rarer.

For sleeping in the cliff
is the barely lit skull,
the claw hangs in the claw
in the dark stone, and the stigmata
are healed in the violet of the volcano.

Of the great storms of light,
none has come to life.

So nehm ich vom Salz,
wenn uns das Meer übersteigt,
und kehre zurück
und legs auf die Schwelle
und trete ins Haus.

Wir teilen ein Brot mit dem Regen,
ein Brot, eine Schuld und ein Haus.

So I gather the salt
when the sea overcomes us,
and turn back
and lay it on the threshold
and step into the house.

We share bread with the rain;
bread, a debt, and a house.

Große Landschaft bei Wien

Geister der Ebene, Geister des wachsenden Stroms,
zu unsrem Ende gerufen, haltet nicht vor der Stadt!
Nehmt auch mit euch, was vom Wein überhing
auf brüchigen Rändern, und führt an ein Rinnsal,
wen nach Ausweg verlangt, und öffnet die Steppen!

Drüben verkümmert das nackte Gelenk eines Baums,
ein Schwungrad springt ein, aus dem Feld schlagen
die Bohrtürme den Frühling, Statuenwäldern weicht
der verworfene Torso des Grüns, und es wacht
die Iris des Öls über den Brunnen im Land.

Was liegt daran? Wir spielen die Tänze nicht mehr.
Nach langer Pause: Dissonanzen gelichtet, wenig cantabile.
(Und ihren Atem spür ich nicht mehr auf den Wangen!)
Still stehn die Räder. Durch Staub und Wolkenspreu
schleift den Mantel, der unsre Liebe deckte, das Riesenrad.

Nirgends gewährt man, wie hier, vor den ersten Küssen
die letzten. Es gilt, mit dem Nachklang im Mund
weiterzugehn und zu schweigen. Wo der Kranich
im Schilf der flachen Gewässer seinen Bogen vollendet,
tönender als die Welle, schlägt ihm die Stunde im Rohr.

Asiens Atem ist jenseits.

Rhythmischer Aufgang von Saaten, reifer Kulturen
Ernten vorm Untergang, sind sie verbrieft, so weiß ichs
dem Wind noch zu sagen. Hinter der Böschung
trübt weicheres Wasser das Aug, und es will
mich noch anfallen trunkenes Limesgefühl;

Great Landscape Near Vienna

Spirits of the plain, spirits of the swelling river,
called for our end, don't halt before the city!
Take also with you whatever wine spilled over
the fragile banks and lead to a channel
whoever demands an exit, and open the plains!

Nearby there shrivels the naked knot of a tree,
a flywheel starts spinning, the derricks pump
spring from the fields, erected forests macerate
the degraded torso of greenness, and an iris of oil
watches over the wells of the land.

To what purpose? We dance the dances no longer.
After a long pause: dissonances made clear, barely cantabile.
(And I no longer feel their breath upon my cheeks!)
The wheels stand still. Through dust and cloud husks
the ferris wheel trails the coat that covered our love.

Nowhere does one grant, as here, the last kisses before
the first. We carry the aftertaste in our mouths
and must go on in silence. Where the crane completes
its circle amid the rushes of the marsh's flat water,
on a reed the hour strikes more resonantly than waves.

Asia's breath lies beyond the river.

The rhythmic sprouting of seeds, the harvest of cultures
before their decline, they've been documented, but I can
still speak of them to the wind. Behind the escarpment,
softer water dulls the eye, and the drunken feeling
of Limes' fortified boundaries can still take hold of me;

unter den Pappeln am Römerstein grab ich
nach dem Schauplatz vielvölkriger Trauer,
nach dem Lächeln Ja und dem Lächeln Nein.

Alles Leben ist abgewandert in Baukästen,
neue Not mildert man sanitär, in den Alleen
blüht die Kastanie duftlos, Kerzenrauch
kostet die Luft nicht wieder, über der Brüstung
im Park weht so einsam das Haar, im Wasser
sinken die Bälle, vorbei an der Kinderhand
bis auf den Grund, und es begegnet
das tote Auge dem blauen, das es einst war.

Wunder des Unglaubens sind ohne Zahl.
Besteht ein Herz darauf, ein Herz zu sein?
Träum, daß du rein bist, heb die Hand zum Schwur,
träum dein Geschlecht, das dich besiegt, träum
und wehr dennoch mystischer Abkehr im Protest.
Mit einer andern Hand gelingen Zahlen
und Analysen, die dich entzaubern.
Was dich trennt, bist du. Verström,
komm wissend wieder, in neuer Abschiedsgestalt.

Dem Orkan voraus fliegt die Sonne nach Westen,
zweitausend Jahre sind um, und uns wird nichts bleiben.
Es hebt der Wind Barockgirlanden auf,
es fällt von den Stiegen das Puttengesicht,
es stürzen Basteien in dämmernde Höfe,
von den Kommoden die Masken und Kränze . . .

Nur auf dem Platz im Mittagslicht, mit der Kette
am Säulenfuß und dem vergänglichsten Augenblick
geneigt und der Schönheit verfallen, sag ich mich los
von der Zeit, ein Geist unter Geistern, die kommen.

under the poplars I dig by a Roman stone,
searching for the theater of many peopled grief,
for the smile of Yes and the smile of No.

All life has migrated to the tenements,
new misery is eased sanitarily; in the avenues
the chestnuts blossom scentlessly; the air no longer
smells of candle smoke; over the balustrade
in the park, the hair sways so lonesome; in the water
the balls sink, dropping from the child's hand
to the bottom, until the dead eye encounters
the blue one that it once was.

The wonders of disbelief are innumerable.
Does a heart insist on being a heart?
Dream that you are pure, lift your hand to swear,
dream your lineage, which masters you, dream
and yet still, in protest, resist the mystic's retreat.
In a different manner numbers and analyses
win, and they disenchant you.
What separates you, is you. Wash away,
return wise, newly resigned to leaving.

The sun sails ahead of the hurricane in the west;
two thousand years gone, and nothing of us will remain.
The wind blows baroque garlands to tatters,
the cherub's face falls from the steps,
the bastions plunge into darkening courtyards,
from dressers fall the masks and wreathes. . .

Only in the square, in midday light, chained to
the column's base and toward the most fleeting moment
inclined and seized by beauty, do I break loose
from time, a spirit among spirits arriving.

Maria am Gestade –
das Schiff ist leer, der Stein ist blind,
gerettet ist keiner, getroffen sind viele,
das Öl will nicht brennen, wir haben
alle davon getrunken – wo bleibt
dein ewiges Licht?

So sind auch die Fische tot und treiben
den schwarzen Meeren zu, die uns erwarten.
Wir aber mündeten längst, vom Sog
anderer Ströme ergriffen, wo die Welt
ausblieb und wenig Heiterkeit war.
Die Türme der Ebene rühmen uns nach,
daß wir willenlos kamen und auf den Stufen
der Schwermut fielen und tiefer fielen,
mit dem scharfen Gehör für den Fall.

Maria am Gestade –
the nave is empty, the stone is blind,
no one is saved, many are stricken,
the oil will not burn, we have all
drunk from it – where remains
your eternal light?

And so the fish are also dead and float
towards the black seas that await us.
But we were washed away long ago, gripped
by the pull of other streams, where the world
failed to surface and there was little cheer.
The towers of the plain sing our praises,
because we unconsciously came, falling on the rungs
of depression, then falling deeper,
with an ear sharply tuned for the fall.

Ein Monolog des Fürsten Myschkin
zu der Ballettpantomime ›Der Idiot‹

*Mit puppenhaften Schritten treten die Personen des Spiels
– Parfíon Rogoschin, Nastassia Filipowna, Totzki, Ganja
Iwolgin, General Epantschin und Aglaja -- auf. Die Panto-
mime endet mit dem Schlußtakt der Intrada, und Fürst
Myschkin tritt in die Mitte der Szene. Er spricht den gan-
zen Monolog ohne Musik.*

Ich habe das Wort, ich nahm's
aus der Hand der Trauer,
unwürdig, denn wie sollte ich
würdiger sein als einer der andern –
selbst ein Gefäß für jene Wolke,
die vom Himmel fiel und in uns tauchte,
schrecklich und fremd
und teilhaft der Schönheit
und jeder Verächtlichkeit dieser Welt.

(O Qual der Helle, Qual
des Fiebers, nah an anderen Fiebern,
unsrer gerechten Krankheit
gemeinsamer Schmerz!)

Laß den stummen Zug durch mein Herz gehen,
bis es dunkel wird
und, was mich erleuchtet,
wieder zurückgegeben ist
an das Dunkel.

Wahrhaftig, weil dieser Schmerz
in euch ist, tut ihr,

A Monologue of Prince Myshkin
to the Ballet Pantomime "The Idiot"

Walking like puppets, the characters of the play enter – Parfyon
Rogozhin, Nastasya Filippovna, Totski, Ganya Ivolgin, General
Epanchin and Aglaia. The pantomime ends with the last measure
of the Prelude as Prince Myshkin steps into the middle of the
scene. He speaks the entire monologue without music.

I have the word, I took it
from the hand of sorrow,
unworthy, for how could I
be more worthy than the next –
myself a vessel for that cloud
that fell from the sky, plunging into us,
terrible and strange
and sharing the beauty
and all that's contemptible in this world.

(O torment of light, torment
of the fever, similar to other fevers,
the indiscriminate illness
of our common pain!)

Let the silent thrust pass through my heart
until it becomes dark
and what sets me alight
again is given back
to the darkness.

Truly, because this pain exists
in all of you, you do

was ihr für euer Leben tut,
nicht für euer Leben,
und was ihr zu eurer Ehre tut,
geschieht nicht zu eurer Ehre.

In der Dämonen Gelächter gebrannt,
bodenlos, sind die Schalen
dieses glücklosen Lebens,
das bis zum Rand uns bedenkt.
Trifft eine die andre, so klingen
sie nicht, denn kein Einhalt
ist den Tränen geboten, sprachlos
stürzen sie ab, von Grund
zu Grund, und es verweigert
der letzte, in den sie vergehn,
sich immer unsrem Gehör.
O Stummheit der Liebe!

Jetzt nimmt er jede Person, die er nennt, an der Hand.

Parfion Rogoschin, der Kaufmannssohn,
weiß nichts von einer Million.
In den Winternächten hält sein Gespann
vor den käuflichen Straßen der Welt
und kann sie nicht fahren.
Er schüttet sein Geld in den Schnee,
denn der Schnee ist das Maß

deiner Wangen, Nastassia Filipowna,
dein Name ist eine gefährliche Kurve
in jedem Mund, sie sagen, am Schnee
nähmst du das Maß für deine Wangen,
in deinem Haar wohnten die Winde,
(ich sage nicht: sie sind launisch),
dein Aug sei ein Hohlweg,

what you do for your lives,
and not for the sake of your lives,
and what you do in the name of honor
does nothing for your honor.

Fired by the laughter of demons,
the bottomless drinking cups
of this unfortunate life
study us to the very end.
If one cup strikes another, they make
no sound, for no end to the tears
is ordered, as speechless
they fall from realm
to realm, the last one,
in which they cease, denied
to us and our hearing.
O the muteness of love!

He takes by the hand each person that he names.

Parfyon Rogozhin, the merchant's son,
cares nothing about a million rubles.
During winter nights, he halts his team
before the affordable streets of the world,
but he cannot drive through them.
He tosses his money into the snow,
for snow is the essence

of your cheeks, Nastasya Filippovna,
your name a dangerous curve
in every mouth, for they say from snow
you took the measure for your cheeks,
in your hair lived the winds,
(I wouldn't say so: they're merely fickle)
your eye could be the gorge

in dem ihre Wagen stürzen,
es zählt sie der Schnee, und vom Schnee
erhältst du das Maß
für deine Wangen.

Totzki – dies ist wohl zuviel,
eh man zur Ruhe geht: eines Kindes Augenblick
in den Armen war die Vergangenheit, und jetzt
ist die Zeit von Blicken, die Zeit
von Lippen über euch beide gekommen.

Ganja Iwolgin, wenn ein Band zwischen allen
gesponnen ist,
werden deine Hände die Knoten sein,
die es spannen,
denn du lächelst nicht gut.
Du forderst zu viel für dich
und verlangst zu wenig von dir.
Dich gängelt nur ein Verlangen:
die Wagen stürzen zu sehn,
in denen die anderen fahren,
eh du selbst unter Rädern verendest.

General Epantschin – es sind nicht Zufälle,
die uns in die Nähe derer führen, die wir meiden.
Wie wir uns in den Kindern entgleiten,
gleiten wir uneingestandenen Wünschen nach
und halten vor fremden Türen als Hüter,
die wir uns selbst so wenig zu hüten vermögen.

Was aber entglitt? Der weiße,
erkaltete Traum einer Jugend,
die nicht Nachsicht verlangt?

into which their carriages will plunge
because of the snow, and from the snow
you received the measure
of your cheeks.

Totski — this is much too much
before one's final rest: the past was a moment
held like a babe in arms, and now
the time of glancing eyes, the time
of lips has taken hold of both of you.

Ganya Ivolgin, when a cord is stretched
between everyone,
your hands will be the knots
that tighten it,
for you don't laugh easily.
You want too much for yourself
and ask too little from yourself.
Only one desire leads you on:
to see the carriages plunge
in which the others ride
before you are crushed under the wheels.

General Epanchin — it's no accident
that led us into your realm, which now we shun.
Just as something of us passes on to our children,
we succumb to inadmissable desires
and stand as guards before strange doors
which we ourselves are so incapable of guarding.

But what slipped away? The white,
chilly dream of youth
that asks for no leniency?

Vollkommenes also? Und Schönheit
in solcher Gestalt, daß wir uns
mit ihrem Rätsel begnügen? Aglaja,
so werde ich in dir nichts sehen
als die Botschaft einer Welt,
in die ich nicht eintreten,
ein Versprechen, das ich nicht halten,
und einen Besitz, den ich nicht wahren kann.

*Er wendet sich um und steht mit dem Gesicht zum
Publikum.*

Erwacht zum Leben im Schein,
von Planeten verführt,
die von uns Ausdruck verlangen,
seh ich zur grenzenlosen Musik
die Bewegung der Stummen.

*Hier münden seine Worte in einen marionettenhaft starren
Tanz.*

Unsere Schritte sind nur die wenig
genauen Anschläge weniger Töne,
die uns erreichen.

*In den Tanz, der die Einsamkeit jedes einzelnen zum Aus-
druck bringen soll, wird auch Myschkin hineingezogen.*

Or perfection? And beauty
rendered such that we've
had enough of its puzzle? Aglaia,
I will see nothing in you
but the message of a world
into which I cannot enter,
a promise, which I cannot keep,
a possession, which I cannot protect.

He turns and faces the audience.

Awakened to life in the radiance
that traveled from the planets
that depend on us to name them,
I witness borderless music
in the movement of the mute.

Here his words accompany a stiff marionette dance.

Our steps are only the few
precise strokes of the even fewer tones
that reach us.

*Myshkin is drawn into a dance in which the loneliness of
each character is expressed.*

Ein Interieur, das die Atmosphäre einer Zirkusarena schafft. Nastassia gängelt Totzki, Ganja und den General an weißen Bändern und spielt in einem tragischen, gewagten, gefährlichen Tanz ihre Macht über die drei Männer aus. Dann erscheint Rogoschin, und Nastassia dreht sich an den Männern vorbei. Ihr Kostüm fällt stückweise von ihr ab, so daß sie zuletzt, nur mit einem weißen Trikot bekleidet, unter einer goldenen Kugel steht. Sie hebt eine Hand zum Ball und reicht die andere Rogoschin, der abwartend abseits gestanden ist. In diesem Augenblick tritt Myschkin auf sie zu.

Halt ein! Dich beschwör ich,
Gesicht der einzigen Liebe,
bleib hell und schlag mit den Wimpern
das Auge zur Welt zu, bleib schön,
Gesicht der einzigen Liebe,
und heb deine Stirn
aus dem Wetterleuchten der Zweifel.
Deine Küsse werden sie teilen,
dich entstellen im Schlaf,
wenn du nach Spiegeln blickst,
in denen du jedem gehörst!

Myschkin führt Nastassia zur Vorderbühne und steigt mit ihr in ein Trapez, das aus dem Schnürboden herabgelassen wurde. Während die beiden langsam in die Höhe schweben, erklingen nur wenige Takte einer sehr zarten Musik.

Sei wahr und gib dem Schnee die Jahre zurück,
nimm Maß an dir selbst und laß die Flocken
dich nur von ungefähr streifen.

An interior that gives off the atmosphere of a circus arena. Nastasya leads around Totski, Ganya, and the General on white cords and expresses her power over the three men in a tragic, bold, dangerous dance. Then Rogozhin appears and Nastasya turns away from the three men. Her costume falls off her piece by piece, so that she stands finally under a golden ball dressed only in white tights. She lifts one hand to the ball and gives the other to Rogozhin, who stands waiting at her side. At this moment, Myshkin steps up to them.

Stop! I beg of you,
face of my only love,
stay lovely, and with your lashes, shut
out the world, stay beautiful,
face of my only love,
and turn your brow
from the heat lightning of doubt.
They will share your kisses,
disfigure you when you are asleep,
when you glance in the mirror
in which you belong to everyone!

Myshkin leads Nastasya downstage and climbs with her into a trapeze that is lowered from above. As they both swing slowly through the air, only a few bars of very tender music are heard.

Be true and give the years back to the snow,
take measure of yourself and let the flakes
strike you only now and then.

Auch dies ist die Welt:
ein früher Stern, den wir als Kinder
bewohnen; verteilt an die Brunnen
als Inhalt und Regen der Stunden,
als Vorrat von heiterer Zeit.
Auch dies ist schon Geist, eines armen
fröhlichen Spiels Einerlei, die Schaukel
im Wind und ein Lachen oben und unten;
dies ist das Ziel, von uns selbst
nicht besessen zu sein
und jedes Ziel zu verfehlen;
und auch dies ist Musik,
mit einem törichten Ton,
immer demselben,
einem Lied nachzugehen,
das uns ein spätres verspricht.

Fall nicht in den Tumult des Orchesters,
in dem die Welt sich verspielt.
Du stürzt, wenn du jetzt deinen Bogen
vergibst, und redest mit deinem Fleisch
eine vergängliche Sprache.

Doch Nastassia gleitet vom Trapez in Rogoschins Arme.

The world is also this:
a former star, which as children
we inhabited; casting it into the fountain
as the content and rain of hours,
as the remains of a brighter time.
This is also the spirit, a poor,
merry game of monotony, the swing swaying
in the wind, laughter above and below;
this is the goal, not to be
obsessed with ourselves
and to give up every goal;
and this is also the music,
with its foolish tone,
always the same,
pursuing a song
that promises us a later one.

Don't fall into the orchestra's tumult
in which the world plays itself out.
You'll plummet if you toss away your bow
and speak with your flesh
a fleeting speech.

Nastasya slips from the trapeze into Rogozhin's arms.

Vor einer riesigen roten Ikone steht eine Leiter, auf der
Myschkin sitzt. Rogoschin liegt rücklings auf einer Prit-
sche, hört mit zunehmender Spannung der Erzählung
Myschkins zu und beobachtet erregt, wie Myschkin lang-
sam von der Leiter heruntersteigt.

Jedem meiner Augenblicke zähle ich einen fremden
Augenblick zu, den Augenblick eines Menschen,
den ich in mir verborgen trage zu jeder Zeit,
und sein Gesicht in diesem Augenblick,
das ich nie vergessen werde, mein Leben lang nicht.

(Kein Gesicht, das abends von innen reift!)
Bedeckt vom Reif einer Kerkernacht
und frostgrün, weht es dem Morgen entgegen,
mit dem Gitter über den Augen, die doch dem Himmel
einmal aufgetan waren.

Durch die kalten Gänge der Glieder verläßt den Gefangenen
    der Schlaf.
Die Schritte des Wärters hallen in seiner Brust.
Ein Schlüssel sperrt seinen Seufzern auf.

Weil er keine Worte hat,
weil keiner ihn versteht,
bringt man ihm Fleisch und Wein
und übt Nächstenliebe an ihm.

Er aber, versunken
in die Zeremonien des Ankleidens,
kann Wohltaten nicht begreifen,
auch nichts von der Vermessenheit
dessen, was befohlen ist.

Before a huge red icon there stands a ladder on which Myshkin sits. Rogozhin lies behind it on a plank bed, listening intently to Myshkin's story and watching in agitation as Myshkin climbs down slowly from the top of the ladder.

In each of my moments, I'm aware of a strange
moment, the moment of a person
whom I carry concealed for every occasion,
as well as his face within this moment,
which I will never forget my entire life.

(Not the face that blossoms for them nightly!)
Covered with the frost of a prison night
and itself frost green, it floats before morning
with bars before the eyes that nonetheless once
were opened to the sky.

Through the cold halls of each wing, sleep abandons
   the prisoner.
The warden's footsteps echo in his chest.
A key unlocks his sighs.

Because he has no word,
because no one understands him,
he is brought meat and wine
so charity can be practiced on him.

But he, sunk within
the ceremony of simply dressing,
cannot appreciate good deeds,
nor the audacity
of what has been ordered.

Es beginnt ja ein langes Leben,
wenn die Tür aufgeht und offen bleibt,
wenn die Straßen in Straßen
münden und das Gefälle der Stimmen
des ganzen Volkes ihn hinunterträgt
an die Gestade des Blutmeers,
das von den verbrecherischen
Gerichten der ganzen Welt
mit Todesurteilen
gespeist wird.

Nun ist aber eine Gemeinsamkeit zwischen uns
und dem Urteil, das auch sagt, daß dieser Mann
mit einem vollkommen wahren Gesicht zu der einen
Wahrheit kommt, eh er den Kopf
genau auf das Brett legt
(obwohl sein Gesicht
weiß ist und ohne Bewegung,
und die Gedanken, die er denken mag,
sind vielleicht ohne Bedeutung, er sieht
nur den rostigen Knopf an der Jacke
des Scharfrichters).

Eine Gemeinsamkeit ist auch zwischen uns
und dem Verurteilten, da er uns zu überzeugen vermag,
daß dem Mord, den wir bereiten,
und dem Mord, der für uns bereitet wird,
die Wahrheit vorangeht.
Und es liegt einer vor mir,
und ich stehe vor einem
mit allen Möglichkeiten zu dieser Wahrheit
und mit dem Mut zu ihrem Leben
und zu unserem Tode.

No doubt a long life begins
when the door opens and stays open,
when the streets flow into
streets and the cascade of voices
from all the people carries him
down to the bank of the sea of blood,
which by the corrupt courts
of the entire world
will be fed sentences
of death.

But now there is a commonness between us
and the sentence that also says this man,
with a completely honest face, attains
the one truth, before he lays his head
precisely upon the block
(although his face
is white and motionless,
and the thoughts he likes to think
are perhaps without meaning, he sees
the bloody head on the jacket
of the executioner).

There's also a commonness between us
and the sentenced, for he can convince us
that the murder, for which we prepare,
and the murder, which for us is prepared,
is preceded by the truth.
And one lies before me,
and I stand before another
with all the possibilities of this truth
and with the courage for its life
and our death.

Doch in meiner Sterblichkeit
kann ich nichts lehren
und könnt' ich's, so selbst
nur in dem Augenblick, von dem ich spreche,
und ich hätte in diesem Augenblick
nichts mehr zu sagen.

Jetzt springt Rogoschin auf und wirft Myschkin, der gegen Ende der Erzählung die unterste Sprosse erreicht hat, zu Boden. Es erklingt wieder die sehr zarte Musik. Verwandelt geht Rogoschin auf Myschkin zu, hebt ihn auf und hält ihn in den Armen. Sie tauschen ihre Kreuze.

Yet in my mortality
I can teach nothing, and even
if I could, it would only be
at the moment in which I speak,
and at this moment I would
have nothing more to say.

Rogozhin jumps up and throws Myshkin to the ground just as he reaches the bottom rung. Again, very tender music starts up. Transformed, Rogozhin goes to Myshkin, lifts him up, and holds him in his arms. They exchange crosses.

Auf der leeren schwarzen Bühne ist in ganz dünnen, wei-
ßen Umrissen ein schloßartiges Haus aufgebaut. Durch das
Haus ist eine gleichfalls weiße Ballettstange gezogen, an
der Aglaja, in ein blendend weißes Tutu gekleidet, steht.
Myschkin, der die Variation auf Puschkins Ballade vom
armen Ritter auf der Vorderbühne mit dem Gesicht zum
Publikum spricht, dreht sich zu Aglaja kein einziges Mal
um, die jedes Mal, wenn der Text von der Musik – einem
Ritornell – unterbrochen wird, an der Ballettstange ein kri-
stallklares Ballettexercise vollbringt. Die Szene beginnt mit
Musik.

Bürgschaft übernehm ich für einen,
der auf dieser Welt lebte vor langer Zeit
und als sonderbar galt, einen Ritter,
aber wie nenn ich ihn heute,
da's kein Verdienst ist, in Armut
und nicht auf Schlössern zu leben?

Sorglos kleidete er sich in die Tage,
bis einer um seine Schultern
franste und ihm ein Licht
auflud, in dessen Umkreis
die Scham nicht geduldet war
und der endliche Friede der Langmut.

Die den Krieg verdammen, sind auserwählt,
zu kämpfen in diesem Licht.
Sie streuen das Korn
auf die toten Äcker der Welt,
sie liegen in den Feuerlinien
einen Sommer lang,
sie binden die Garben für uns
und fallen im Wind.

On the empty black stage there stands the skeletal white frame of
a palatial house. Made of the same material as the house frame, a
white ballet bar runs through the house, at which stands Aglaia
dressed in a bright white tutu. Myshkin, who speaks the variation
on Pushkin's "Ballad of the Poor Knight" while facing the audience
downstage, never once turns to Aglaia. Meanwhile, every time the
music score — a ritornelle — is interrupted, she completes a very
precise ballet exercise at the bar. The scene begins with music.

I put up bail for one
who lived in this world long ago
and was exceptional as a knight,
but what should I call him today,
given there's little merit in living
in poverty and not in castles?

Without worry he draped the day
around his shoulders, until
one day he stood fringed by an aura
of radiant light, in whose circle
shame was not tolerated,
nor the quiet reserve of patience.

Those who damn the war are chosen
to battle in this light.
They scatter the grain
on the dead fields of the world,
they lie in the firing lines
all summer long,
they bind the sheaves for us
and float away upon the wind.

Aglaja wiederholt zum ersten Teil des Ritornells ihre Variation.

In der Zeit der Vorbereitung mied ich die Städte
und lebte gefährlich, wie man es aus Liebe tut.

Später geriet ich in eine Abendgesellschaft
und erzählte von einer Hinrichtung. So fehlte ich abermals.

Meinen ersten Tod empfing ich aus der Hand eines
    Gewitters
und ich dachte: so hell ist die Welt und so außer sich,

wo ich die Wiesen verdunkle, schaufelt der Wind Erde
über ein Kreuz, laßt mich liegen mit dem Gesicht nach
    unten!

Blaue Steine flogen nach mir und erweckten mich vom
    Tode.
Sie rührten von einem Sternengesicht, das zerbrach.

Aglaja wiederholt zum ersten Teil des Ritornells ihre Variation.

Und ausgestoßen aus dem Orden der Ritter,
verwiesen aus den Balladen,
nehme ich einen Weg durch die Gegenwart,
zu auf den Horizont, wo die zerrissenen
Sonnen im Staub liegen,
wo die Schattenspiele
auf der unerhörten Wand des Himmels
zu Verwandlungen greifen und ihr
einen Stoff einbilden
aus dem alten
Glauben meines Kindergebets.

Aglaia repeats her variation to the first part of the ritornelle.

During training, I avoided the cities
and lived on the run, like someone in love.

Later I turned up at an evening party
and told of an execution. I felt out of place again.

I received my first death from the hand of a thunderbolt
and I thought: the world is so bright and exceptional;

where I darken the fields, the wind shoveled earth
over a cross, allowing me to lie with my face down!

Blue stones flew at me and awakened me from death.
They came from the face of a star that had shattered.

Aglaia repeats her variation to the first part of the ritornelle.

And banished from the order of knights,
exiled from the ballads,
I follow a path through the present
to the horizon, where ragged suns
lie in the dust,
where the play of shadows
on the unknown wall of heaven
grasps the transformation and creates
a substance for it
out of the old beliefs
of my childhood prayers.

Wenn auch die Kränze entzwei sind,
abgesprungen die Perlen, wenn der Kuß
in die blauen Falten der Madonnen,
abgeschmackt nach den Ekstasen
so vieler Nächte, beim ersten Hauch
das Licht in den Nischen löscht,
trete ich aus dem schwarzen
Blut der Ungläubigen in mein eignes
und höre auf den Abgesang
einer Geschichte,
die unsre Opfer verachtet.

Aglaja wiederholt zum ersten Teil des Ritornells ihre Variation.

Mir will eine Schwäche, der Wahnsinn
willkommen ist, meinen Weg
vertreten und mich der Freiheit entziehn.

Hörig dem Sog, wich mein Fleisch
früh den Messern aus, die ich hob,
um es aufzureißen. Mit dem Hauch,
den es umklammert, will es hinab,
mit meinem Atem, den ich zurückgeben werde
zum Beweis, daß mein Mund
nicht gefragt hat nach meinem Leben
und den Bedingungen, unter denen
wir für die Schöpfung
zu zeugen haben.

Mit dem zweiten Teil des Ritornells endet die Szene, und Aglaja erstarrt auf der Spitze, in der letzten ihrer Attituden.

Even if the garlands were broken in two
and the pearls fell off, if the kiss
placed in the blue folds of the Madonna
were tasteless after the ecstasies
of so many nights, or like the first breath
of the candles blown out in niches,
I would step out of the black
blood of the infidel within me
and listen to the final stanza
of a history
that scorns our victims.

Aglaia repeats her variation to the first part of the ritornelle.

A weakness that welcomes madness
wants to obstruct my path
and take away my freedom.

Vulnerable to its pull, my flesh
soon learned to avoid the knife I raised
to cut it open. With the breath
that they surround, my lungs collapse
with the breath that I will give back,
this being the evidence that my mouth
didn't ask about my life
and the conditions under which
we were witnesses
to the Creation.

*The scene ends with the second part of the ritornelle, and Aglaia
freezes on the tip of a toe and in her final position.*

Wir sehen eine Kurpromenade mit einem Orchestertempel-chen im Hintergrund. Eine Gesellschaft von Vögeln hat sich hier versammelt – gemeint ist die Petersburger Haute-volee. Wenn der Vorhang sich öffnet, hält der Dirigent der kleinen Kapelle den Taktstock hoch. Die Vogelgesellschaft steht regungslos. Jeder ist in seiner Pose erstarrt, so daß die Szene den Eindruck eines kolorierten Druckes macht. Im Vordergrund steht Myschkin, der sich sehr fremd in dieser Umgebung fühlt.

Die leicht fliegen, werde ich nicht
beneiden, die Gesellschaft der Vögel,
die viele Orte berührt
und noch im raschesten Flug
voll Überdruß ist.

Myschkin geht ab. Der Dirigent des kleinen Orchesters be-wegt seinen Taktstock zur Musik, und die erstarrte Vogel-gesellschaft löst sich in eine »Kurpromenade« auf. Wenn die Musik endet, wenden sich alle dem Kapellmeister zu und applaudieren. Etwas vor Schluß des Tanzes treten Myschkin und Aglaja auf. Sie nehmen an dem Treiben teil und gehen dann zur Vorderbühne. Und Myschkin erklärt sich Aglaja.

Wo ich hinkam, fand ich mich unter Steinen,
wie sie ergraut und von Vertrauen befangen.

Mir ist gewiß, daß auch dein Gesicht
so alt herabfiel und sich neben mich legte
unter den eisweißen Wasserfall,
unter dem ich zuerst mein Bett aufschlug
und unter dem ich in meinem Tode
liegen werde, den Absturz
der Reinheit vor Augen.

We see a resort promenade with a bandstand in the background. A Society of Birds has assembled here, meaning the cream of Petersburg's society. As the curtain rises, the conductor of the tiny band holds the baton high. The Society of Birds stands by motionless. Each is frozen in his or her pose, so the scene gives the impression of a colored print. Myshkin stands downstage, feeling very strange in these surroundings.

Those who flit about, I will not
envy, namely the Society of Birds
that touch down in many places,
though in their hasty flight
they are still full of ennui.

Myshkin departs. The conductor of the tiny band moves his baton to the music, and the frozen society begins to move about in a promenade. As the music ends, they all turn to the band leader and applaud. Just before the end of the dance, Myshkin and Aglaia enter. They take part in the proceedings and then come downstage. Myshkin speaks to Aglaia.

When I came to, I found myself mingling with stones.
I turned as gray as they and felt full of trust.

I'm certain that also your face
has become old and has lain next to me
under the ice cold waterfall,
under which I first laid out my bed,
and under which I will lie
in my death, the cascade
of purity before my eyes.

Myschkin und Aglaja gehen ab. Es wird Abend. Einige
Lampions leuchten auf, die Kapelle hört zu spielen auf, die
Gesellschaft findet sich paarweise zusammen und verläßt
die Bühne. Blaue Versatzstücke kommen von oben, und die
Bühne wird von einem klaren Blau überströmt. Dann fliegt
Aglaja herein, von weißen Tänzern gefolgt, und Myschkin
erscheint ihr als Wunschbild in einem weißen Kostüm.
Doch Nastassias Erscheinung tritt zwischen die Liebenden
und trennt sie. Die blauen Versatzstücke werden weggeho-
ben. Allein im nächtlichen Garten sieht Aglaja sich er-
nüchtert um und wirft sich weinend auf eine Bank. Mysch-
kin, in realer Gestalt, kommt und kniet vor ihr nieder.

Ich habe Zutrauen gefaßt zum Verzicht.
Du weinst, weil ich dich meinen Wünschen vorziehe?
Du wählst ein kurzes Los: meine Zeit, und ich will
die Verheerungen aller Träume, mit denen
du schläfst und herausreichst aus der Welt.

Für dich habe ich keinen Trost.
Wir werden beisammen liegen,
wenn die Bewegung der Berge geschieht,
mit einem Steingefühl, alterslos,
auf dem Boden der Nachtfurcht
und im Anfang einer großen Verstörung.

Einmal nur hatte der Mond das Nachsehn.
Ins Geäst unsres Herzens
fiel das einsamere
Licht der Liebe.
Wie kalt die Welt ist
und wie rasch die Schatten
sich auf unsre Wurzeln niederlegen!

Myshkin and Aglaia depart. Evening falls. Some street lights are lit, the band stops playing, the Society comes together in twos and moves offstage. A blue background is lowered from above and the stage is lit with a clear blue light. Then Aglaia rushes in followed by dancers in white, and Myshkin appears to her as a dream in a white costume. Yet Nastasya's entrance falls between the two and separates them. The blue background is lifted up and away. Alone in the night garden and disillusioned, Aglaia looks around and throws herself in tears onto the bench. Myshkin, revealing his true character, comes and kneels before her.

I have become resigned to your rejection.
You cry because I prefer you to my own wishes?
You drew a short straw: my time, and I want
the devastation of all the dreams with which
you sleep and which you hand out to the world.

For you I have no comforting words.
We will lie side by side
when the mountains begin to move,
ourselves feeling like stones, timeless,
on the firm ground of night's fear
and at the start of a vast confusion.

Only once the moon was abandoned.
Onto the branches of our heart
fell the lonelier
light of love.
How cold the world is
and how swift the shadows
that lay themselves upon our roots.

Aglaja hört Myschkin verständnislos zu; ihre Erwartungen sind enttäuscht worden, sie springt auf und läßt Myschkin betroffen stehen. Die Vögel kehren in den nächtlichen Garten zurück, diesmal um Nastassia Filipowna versammelt, die durch ihre faszinierende Schönheit in einem herausfordernden Tanz alles in Atem hält. Dann stehen die beiden Frauen voreinander. Nastassia beleidigt Aglaja und wird von einem der Begleiter Aglajas wieder beleidigt. Myschkin geht ab, und die aufgescheuchte Vogelgesellschaft flieht. Das Licht ist auf den Vordergrund gerichtet, während die Kulissen fortgetragen werden; nur ein schwarzumkleidetes Podium mit zwei Seitenleitern bleibt auf der Bühne, und Aglaja und Nastassia tanzen mit schwarzgekleideten Partnern ihre Variationen, als kämpften sie mit unsichtbaren Floretten auf Leben und Tod. Wenn Myschkin zurückkommt, steigen die beiden Frauen auf je eine der Leitern und bedeuten ihm, daß sie seine Erklärung erwarten. Aglaja sieht Myschkins Zögern, wirft sich vom Podium herunter und wird von ihrem Partner weggetragen. Ehe Myschkin ihr folgen kann, bricht Nastassia wie leblos vor ihm zusammen. Er hebt sie auf und hält sie in den Armen.

Aglaia listens disbelieving to Myshkin. Her expectations having been disappointed, she jumps up and lets Myshkin stand there dismayed. The Birds return to the night garden, this time gathering around Nastasya Filippovna, who holds them breathless through her compelling beauty during a provocative dance. Then both women face each other. Nastasya gestures insultingly to Aglaia and is insulted in turn by one of Aglaia's companions. Myshkin departs and the embarrassed Society flees. The light is directed downstage while the scenery is carried off. Only a podium clad in black with a ladder on each side remains on stage, and Aglaia and Nastasya dance their variations with partners dressed in black as if fighting a life or death battle with invisible foils. As Myshkin returns, both women climb up a ladder on each side of the podium and signal to him that they expect an explanation. Aglaia notes Myshkin's hesitation, jumps from the podium, and is carried away by her partner. Before Myshkin can follow her, Nastasya collapses, as if lifeless, before him. He lifts her up and holds her in his arms.

Auf der leeren Bühne stehen, in schwarzen Kostümen, mit
dem Rücken zum Publikum, Menschen mit Kandelabern,
während Myschkin, zum Publikum gewendet, spricht.

Mit einem geliehenen Wort bin ich,
und nicht mit dem Feuer, gekommen
und schuld an allem, o Gott!
Es sind die Kreuze getauscht,
und das eine wird nicht getragen.
Schwach lob ich die Strenge
Deines Gerichts und ich denke
schon an Vergebung, ehe Du sie gewährst.

Wo die Angst in mir aufspringt
und Helle vor mir herwirft, entdeck ich
Schreckliches und meine Schuld
an allem, an dem Verbrechen,
mit dem ich noch diese Nacht
in Deine Nacht kommen muß,
und mein heilloses Wissen will ich
nicht preisgeben an mein Gewissen.

Sei Du die Liebe, ich bin nur in leisem
Fieber aus Dir hervorgegangen
und unter Fiebernden hinfällig
geworden. Deine Blindheit erkennend,
vor der wir eins sind im Dunkel,
bekenn ich, daß ich schuld bin
an allem, denn Du, seit Du uns nicht
mehr siehst, zählst auf ein Wort.

On the empty stage a number of people stand in black costumes,
holding candlelabras and with their backs to the audience as
Myshkin faces the audience and speaks.

With a borrowed word I have come,
and not with the fire, for I am
to blame for everything, O God!
The crosses have been exchanged,
but one will not be worn.
Weakly I praise the severity
of Your justice, and already I hope
for pardon before You even grant it.

Where fear leaps up inside me
and blinding light opens before me, I discover
the horror and my guilt
for everything, for the crime
with which, on this night,
into Your night I must come,
though I don't want to relinquish
my wretched knowledge to my belief.

Let it be that You are Love, for I am only
a light fever that came from You,
one who, between the delirium, became
frail. Knowing Your blindness,
before which we are as one in darkness,
I acknowledge that I'm guilty
of everything, for You, since You no longer
see us, depend upon a word.

Ein roter Teppich wird herausgerollt. Myschkin dreht sich um und steht jetzt auch mit dem Rücken zum Publikum. Nastassia erscheint und versucht, auf die Vorderbühne zu Myschkin zu gelangen, doch Rogoschin springt einige Male, mit einem Messer in der Hand, dazwischen. Die schwarzen Gestalten führen an Ort und Stelle entsprechende Schritte zu einem Bolero aus. Schließlich ergreift Rogoschin Nastassia und trägt sie, mit dem Rücken zum Publikum, von der Bühne. Auch die schwarzen Gestalten gehen ab. Die Ikone senkt sich aus dem Schnürboden herunter. Myschkin steht ohnmächtig davor.

Öffne mir!
Alle Tore sind zugefallen, es ist Nacht,
und was zu sagen ist, ist noch nicht gesagt.
Öffne mir!
Die Luft ist voll von Verwesung, und mein Mund
hat den blauen Mantel noch nicht geküßt.
Öffne mir!
Ich lese schon in den Linien deiner Hand, mein Geist,
der meine Stirne berührt und mich heimholen will.
Öffne mir!

Endlich tritt Rogoschin heraus, und Myschkin geht ihm entgegen.

Geheim ist der Mund, mit dem ich morgen rede. Ich will diese Nacht mit dir wachen und werde dich nicht verraten.

Behutsam führt Rogoschin Myschkin hinter die Ikone. Die Bühne wird ganz dunkel, und im Dunkeln spricht Myschkin die beiden Terzinen.

A red carpet is rolled out. Myshkin turns around and stands with his back to the audience as well. Nastasya appears, looks for Myshkin, and tries to go to him downstage, but Rogozhin springs between them a few times with a knife in his hand. The figures in black perform steps that correspond to a bolero right where they stand. Finally, Rogozhin carries off Nastasya with his back to the audience. The figures in black also depart. The icon is lowered from above. Myshkin stands powerless before it.

Open the door!
All gates are closed, it is night,
and what must be said has not been said.
Open the door!
The air is full of decay, and my mouth
has not yet kissed the blue cloak.
Open the door!
Spirit, who touches my forehead and wants
to take me home, I can read the lines of your hand.
Open the door!

Finally Rogozhin steps forward and Myshkin towards him.

Sealed is the mouth with which I'll speak tomorrow.
I want to wake with you tonight and not betray you.

Rogozhin leads Myshkin behind the icon with care. The stage becomes completely dark, and in darkness Myshkin speaks both tercets.

In den Strängen der Stille hängen die Glocken
und läuten den Schlaf ein,
so schlafe, sie läuten den Schlaf ein.

In den Strängen der Stille kommen die Glocken
zur Ruhe, es könnte der Tod sein,
so komm, es muß Ruhe sein.

*Es wird etwas hell. Aus dem Schnürboden kommen weiße
Stricke zu den Klängen der Apotheose herab. Myschkin
bleibt unbeweglich stehen, und während immer mehr
Stricke herabsinken, erscheinen Tänzer, die in verhaltenen,
feierlichen Bewegungen den Ausbruch des Wahnsinns dar-
stellen.*

Choreographie: Tatjana Gsovsky
Musik: Hans Werner Henze

From the cords of silence hang the bells,
and they toll as a prelude to sleep,
so sleep, they toll as a prelude to sleep.

On the cords of silence finally the bells
keep their peace; this could be death,
so come, there must be peace.

It becomes somewhat brighter. White cords are lowered from above to the strains of an apotheosis. Myshkin remains motionless, and as more and more cords are lowered, dancers appear who, with restrained, solemn movements depict the onset of madness.

Choreography: Tatyana Gsovsky
Music: Hans Werner Henze

Anrufung des Großen Bären

Invocation of the Great Bear

I

Das Spiel ist aus

Mein lieber Bruder, wann bauen wir uns ein Floß
und fahren den Himmel hinunter?
Mein lieber Bruder, bald ist die Fracht zu groß
und wir gehen unter.

Mein lieber Bruder, wir zeichnen aufs Papier
viele Länder und Schienen.
Gib acht, vor den schwarzen Linien hier
fliegst du hoch mit den Minen.

Mein lieber Bruder, dann will ich an den Pfahl
gebunden sein und schreien.
Doch du reitest schon aus dem Totental
und wir fliehen zu zweien.

Wach im Zigeunerlager und wach im Wüstenzelt,
es rinnt uns der Sand aus den Haaren,
dein und mein Alter und das Alter der Welt
mißt man nicht mit den Jahren.

Laß dich von listigen Raben, von klebriger Spinnenhand
und der Feder im Strauch nicht betrügen,
iß und trink auch nicht im Schlaraffenland,
es schäumt Schein in den Pfannen und Krügen.

I

The Game is Over

My dearest brother, when will we build a raft
and sail down through the sky?
My dearest brother, the weight's too much for our craft
and we will sink and die.

My dearest brother, we sketch out on paper
countries and railway lines.
Watch out, close to the set of tracks right here
you'll be blown high by mines.

My dearest brother, to a stake I want to be tied,
raising then a cry.
But out of the valley of death you choose to ride,
and off together we fly.

Awake in the gypsy camp and the desert tent,
the sand runs out of our hair;
your age, my age, and the age of the planet
in years can have no measure.

Don't be fooled by the spider, the clever raven,
or in a bush, the feather;
however, don't eat and drink inside a fool's haven,
lies foam in skillets and pitchers.

Nur wer an der goldenen Brücke für die Karfunkelfee
das Wort noch weiß, hat gewonnen.
Ich muß dir sagen, es ist mit dem letzten Schnee
im Garten zerronnen.

Von vielen, vielen Steinen sind unsre Füße so wund.
Einer heilt. Mit dem wollen wir springen,
bis der Kinderkönig, mit dem Schlüssel zu seinem Reich
    im Mund,
uns holt, und wir werden singen:

Es ist eine schöne Zeit, wenn der Dattelkern keimt!
Jeder, der fällt, hat Flügel.
Roter Fingerhut ist's, der den Armen das Leichentuch
    säumt,
und dein Herzblatt sinkt auf mein Siegel.

Wir müssen schlafen gehn, Liebster, das Spiel ist aus.
Auf Zehenspitzen. Die weißen Hemden bauschen.
Vater und Mutter sagen, es geistert im Haus,
wenn wir den Atem tauschen.

On the golden bridge, only he who might know
the troll's secret word can win.
I'm sorry to say, along with our last snow,
it melted in the garden.

From many stones our feet are sore. One can heal.
Let's hop to the fairy tale king,
for it's in his mouth that the castle key's sealed,
and he'll lead us away to sing:

It is a happy time when the date pit sprouts!
Everyone who falls has wings.
Red foxglove is what hems the poor's shrouds,
and your bud is sealed in my ring.

We must go to sleep, my dearest, the game is over.
Off on tiptoe. Our nightshirts billowing white.
The house is always haunted, say Father and Mother,
when we exchange breaths at night.

Von einem Land,
einem Fluß und den Seen

I

Von einem, der das Fürchten lernen wollte
und fortging aus dem Land, von Fluß und Seen,
zähl ich die Spuren und des Atems Wolken,
denn, so Gott will, wird sie der Wind verwehn!

Zähl und halt ein – sie werden vielen gleichen.
Die Lose ähneln sich, die Odysseen.
Doch er erfuhr, daß wo die Lämmer weiden,
schon Wölfe mit den Fixsternblicken stehn.

Er fühlte seine Welle ausgeschrieben,
eh sie ihn wegtrug und ihm Leid geschah;
sie sprang im See auf und sie schwang die Wiege,
in die sein Sternbild durch die Schleier sah.

Er schüttelte und trat die tauben Nüsse,
den Hummeln schlug er schärfre Töne vor,
und Sonntag war ihm mehr als Glockensüße –
Sonntag war jeder Tag, den er verlor.

Er zog den Karren aus verweichten Gleisen,
von keinem leichten Rädergang verführt,
beim Aufschrei, den die Wasser weiterreichten
an Seen, vom ersten Steinschlag aufgerührt.

Doch sieben Steine wurden sieben Brote,
als er im Zweifel in die Nacht entwich;
er tauchte durch den Duft und streute Krumen
im Gehn für den Verlornen hinter sich.

Of a Land, a River and Lakes

I

Left behind by one who wished to learn of dread
in leaving the land of his birth, a river and lakes,
it's footprints that I count, a breath's own cloud,
which later, as God wills, the wind will take.

Count up, and stop – finding they're much the same.
Each journey has its twin, as well as each destiny.
For, in fact, he learned that beside the grazing lamb
the wolf already stands, eyes fixed and starry.

In waves he felt his destiny was written
before it pulled him out into sorrow's lake;
as the wave sprang up, his cradle was aswim,
his star looked on through veils at the baby awake.

He shook and kicked about the empty nutshells,
he returned sharp tones to the bumblebee's buzz,
and Sunday meant more than sweet, ringing bells –
Sunday meant every day that no longer was.

Out of softened, muddy tracks he pulled his wagon,
never having an easy path he could call his own;
a scream was what, as ripples, the water passed on
across the lake when he threw his first stone.

Yet when, full of doubt, one night he disappeared,
the seven stones turned into seven loaves;
he plunged into the meadow's perfumed air,
scattering crumbs for the lost in forest groves.

Erinnre dich! Du weißt jetzt allerlanden:
wer treu ist, wird im Frühlicht heimgeführt.
O Zeit gestundet, Zeit uns überlassen!
Was ich vergaß, hat glänzend mich berührt.

II

Im Frühlicht rücken Brunnen in die Mitte,
der Pfarrer, das Brevier, der Sonntagsstaat,
die kalten Pfeifen und die schwarzen Hüte,
Leib, Ehr und Gut vor allerhöchsten Rat.

Untätig steht der Fluß, die Weiden baden,
die Königskerzen leuchten bis ins Haus,
das schwere Essen ist schon aufgetragen,
und alle Sprüche gehn auf Amen aus.

Die Nachmittage, hell und ungeheuer –
die Nadel springt im Strumpf, Gewöll zerreißt,
und das Geschirr der Pferde wird gescheuert,
bis eins erklirrt, mit dem Fallada reist.

Die Alten liegen in den dumpfen Stuben,
das Testament im Arm, im zweiten Schlaf,
und ihre Söhne zeugen wortlos Söhne
mit Mägden, die der Gott als Regen traf

Gestillte Lippen und gestillte Augen –
die Raupen hängen eingepuppt im Schrein,
und Dunggeruch steigt mit den Fliegentrauben
bei früher Dämmrung durch die Fenster ein.

Am Abend Stimmenauflauf an den Zäunen,
Andacht und Rosen werden laut zerpflückt,

Remember it now! For you know it's obvious:
who's faithful is led home in the early light.
O borrowed time, the time still left to us!
What I forgot now stirs inside me bright.

II

In early light, the fountains quell their splash,
the parson, the breviary, the Sunday finery,
the pipes extinguished, rows of formal black hats,
body, honor, and goods sit before the Deity.

Still stands the river, beside it willows bask,
the house is bathed by the yellow light of mullein,
as the trays of heavy food are served at last
and all prayers finish with a muttered Amen.

The afternoons so bright and so immense –
the needle darns the sock, dwindling the skein,
outside the horse's harness is being cleansed,
until the buggy sets off with the snap of a rein.

The elderly lie inside their musty dens,
holding the Bible, old couples 'rest their eyes',
as wordlessly their sons beget more sons
with girls who only by rain have been baptized.

Sated eyes and sated lips as well –
caterpillars that hang cocooned in their wrappings;
at dusk, above dung heaps, the flies now circle
wafting the odor through the window's casing.

At evening, voices are gathered by the fence,
prayers and roses are plucked apart with a din,

die Katzen scheuchen auf aus ihren Träumen,
und rote Mieder hat der Wind verrückt.

Die Zöpfe lösen sich, die Schattenpaare
im Nebel auf, vom nahen Hügel rollt
der unfruchtbare Mond, besetzt die Äcker
und nimmt das Land für eine Nacht in Sold.

III

Dem Hügelzug ist eine Burg geblieben,
vom Berg geschützt, der Felsen um sie stellt,
den Geier ausschickt mit dem Krallensiegel,
dem Königswappen, eh sie ganz verfällt.

Es sind drei Tote hinterm Wall verborgen;
von einem weht vom Wachtturm noch das Haar,
von einem heißt es, daß er Steine schleudert,
von einem, daß er doppelköpfig war.

Der stiftet Brand, dem sie zu dritt befehlen,
der mordet, den ein schwarzes Haar umschlingt,
und wer den Stein aufhebt, wird selber sterben,
noch diesen Abend, eh die Amsel singt.

Die unbeschuhten Geister auf den Zinnen,
der unbewehrte Leichnam im Verlies,
im Gästebuch die Namen der Beschauer –
die Nacht vertuscht sie, die uns kommen hieß.

Sie schlägt den Erdplan auf, verschweigt die Ziele;
sie trägt die Zeit als eine Eiszeit ein,
die Schotterstege über die Moränen,
den Weg zu Grauwack und zu Kreidestein.

as cats asleep are frightened from their trance,
and a corset's red flaps madly in the wind.

The pigtails now undone, the pairs of shadows
dissolve in fog, while over the nearest hill
the barren moon now rolls, occupies meadows,
and for a night commands the land at will.

III

There still remains a fortress in the hills
secured by the mountain and the cliffs surrounding
that dispatch vultures, their claws' sharp seals
and coat of arms, as the fortress falls to ruin.

Where atop the tower a corpse's hair still blows,
ensconced behind the wall remain three dead;
of these, the second is known to still sling stones,
while it's said that the third has a pair of heads.

The three together order one to set a fire;
the murderer's the one to whom the black hair clings;
and whoever lifts the stone will himself expire
this very evening before the blackbird sings.

The barefoot spirits that haunt the parapets,
the unarmed corpse that lies within the dungeon,
the guest book filled with names of those who visit —
night sweeps them under, though it still spurs us on.

For night unfolds the map, keeps secret its aim;
it grinds time slowly along, as in an ice age,
the gravel path left by the glacial moraine,
the process that creates both chalk and clay.

Die Drachenzeichnung lobt sie und die Festung,
vom Faltenwurf der frühen Welt umwallt,
wo oben unten war und unten oben.
Die Scholle tanzt noch überm blauen Spalt.

Ins Schwemmland führt die Nacht. Es schwemmt uns wieder
ins Kellerland der kalten neuen Zeit.
So such im Höhlenbild den Traum vom Menschen!
Die Schneehuhnfeder steck dir an das Kleid.

IV

In andren Hüllen gingen wir vorzeiten,
du gingst im Fuchspelz, ich im Iltiskleid;
noch früher waren wir die Marmelblumen,
in einer tiefen Tibetschlucht verschneit.

Wir standen zeitlos, lichtlos in Kristallen
und schmolzen in der ersten Stunde hin,
uns überrann der Schauer alles Lebens,
wir blühten auf, bestäubt vom ersten Sinn.

Wir wanderten im Wunder und wir streiften
die alten Kleider ab und neue an.
Wir sogen Kraft aus jedem neuen Boden
und hielten nie mehr unsren Atem an.

Wir waren leicht als Vögel, schwer als Bäume,
kühn als Delphin und still als Vogelei.
Wir waren tot, lebendig, bald ein Wesen
und bald ein Ding. (Wir werden niemals frei!)

Wir konnten uns nicht halten und wir zogen
in jeden Körper voller Freude ein.

Both fortress and fossil by night are celebrated,
as earlier worlds appear when the curtain lifts,
where down was up, and up was stood on its head.
The firmament still dances above a deep blue rift.

Night settles into alluvium. We're sinking again
into an icy new age's cavernous soil.
Within cave murals look for the dream of man!
Fasten a ptarmigan feather to your lapel.

IV

In earlier times we wandered in other garments,
you in fox fur and I in a polecat skin;
still earlier yet we were flowers of adamant
buried within the snow of a Tibetan ravine.

We stood there timeless, lightless in the crystals,
melting only when the first hour had begun,
and feeling a shiver of life rush over us,
we blossomed, carrying seeds of initial perception.

We wandered within a marvel, shedding old clothes,
donning new clothes later as we moved along.
From each new soil we drew more strength for ourselves,
and never again did we hold our breath so long.

We were light as birds, and as still as their eggs;
we were as bold as dolphins, heavy as trees.
We were dead, yet fully alive — now a being
and now a thing. (We will never be free!)

We could not help changing, and into each body
each of us moved, experiencing our full splendor.

(Und niemand sag ich, was du mir bedeutest —
die sanfte Taube einem rauhen Stein!)

Du liebtest mich. Ich liebte deine Schleier,
die lichten Stoffe, die den Stoff umwehn,
und ohne Neugier hielt ich dich in Nächten.
(Wenn du nur liebst! Ich will dich ja nicht sehn!)

Wir kamen in das Land mit seinen Quellen.
Urkunden fanden wir. Das ganze Land,
so grenzenlos und so geliebt, war unser.
Es hatte Platz in deiner Muschelhand.

V

Wer weiß, wann sie dem Land die Grenzen zogen
und um die Kiefern Stacheldrahtverhau?
Der Wildbach hat die Zündschnur ausgetreten,
der Fuchs vertrieb den Sprengstoff aus dem Bau.

Wer weiß, was sie auf Grat und Gipfel suchten?
Ein Wort? Wir haben's gut im Mund verwahrt;
es spricht sich schöner aus in beiden Sprachen
und wird, wenn wir verstummen, noch gepaart.

Wo anders sinkt der Schlagbaum auf den Pässen;
hier wird ein Gruß getauscht, ein Brot geteilt.
Die Handvoll Himmel und ein Tuch voll Erde
bringt jeder mit, damit die Grenze heilt.

Wenn sich in Babel auch die Welt verwirrte,
man deine Zunge dehnte, meine bog —
die Hauch- und Lippenlaute, die uns narren,
sprach auch der Geist, der durch Judäa zog.

(And I'll tell no one what you mean to me –
as to the rugged stone, the dove so tender!)

It's then you loved me. And I loved your veil,
the luminous light wound through its luminous tulle,
and nightly, absent-minded, it was you I held.
(If you only loved! I have no need to see you!)

We came into this country with its spring waters.
We found deeds they left behind. The entire land
was so open and so loved, all of it ours.
It fit perfectly inside the shell of your hand.

V

Who knows when they divided up the land
with borders, wrapping barbed wire around each fir?
The mountain's roaring stream douses the fuse's brand,
the fox hauls out explosives from his lair.

Who knows just what they sought on summit and ridge?
A word? Inside our mouths it's hidden well away;
it's made more beautiful by each separate language
and will, when we fall silent, still conjugate.

Elsewhere, on mountain passes barriers fall;
here a greeting's exchanged, some bread is shared.
A handful of sky and a pocketful of soil
are brought along so that the border's repaired.

Even though the world became confused in Babel,
your tongue was stretched and also mine was bent –
breath and lip sounds, that still can make us fools,
were spoken by the spirit, who through Judea went.

Seit uns die Namen in die Dinge wiegen,
wir Zeichen geben, uns ein Zeichen kommt,
ist Schnee nicht nur die weiße Fracht von oben,
ist Schnee auch Stille, die uns überkommt.

Daß uns nichts trennt, muß jeder Trennung fühlen;
in gleicher Luft spürt er den gleichen Schnitt.
Nur grüne Grenzen und der Lüfte Grenzen
vernarben unter jedem Nachtwindschritt.

Wir aber wollen über Grenzen sprechen,
und gehn auch Grenzen noch durch jedes Wort:
wir werden sie vor Heimweh überschreiten
und dann im Einklang stehn mit jedem Ort.

VI

Der Schlachttag naht mit hellem Messerwirbel,
die matten Klingen schleift der Morgenwind,
und aus der Brise gehn gestärkt die Schürzen
der Männer, die ums Vieh versammelt sind.

Die Stricke werden fester angezogen,
die Mäuler schäumen, und die Zunge schwimmt;
der Nachbar sorgt für Salz und Pfefferkörner,
und das Gewicht der Opfer wird bestimmt.

Es wollen hier die Toten leichter wiegen,
denn das Lebendige, dem Blut nicht fehlt,
– und mehr als Leben wehrt sich auf der Waage! –
gibt hier den Ausschlag, den kein Zeiger zählt.

Drum meid die Hunde mit den heißen Lefzen
und den Gemeinen, der mit rohem Blut

Since names have cradled us to the nature of things,
since we've posited signs, and to us signs have come;
snow not only means the white weight falling,
snow means the silence by which we're overcome.

To stay together, each must feel separation;
within the same air, he feels the same split within.
Only the borders of air and the borders of green
can be healed at night by each step of the wind.

And yet we are determined to speak across borders,
even if borders pass through every word:
in longing still for home, we will cross over,
and again with every place stand in accord.

VI

With bright knife swirls the day of slaughter nears,
in morning wind the dull knife blades are sharpened,
as around the cattle the men begin to gather,
wearing their aprons that by the breeze are stiffened.

The binding ropes are drawn a little tighter,
muzzles begin to foam, the thick tongues swim;
a neighbor checks his salt and pepper shakers,
while one determines the weight of another victim.

The dead here, in general, tend to weigh much less,
because the living, whose blood is lacking never,
– and what is weighed is more than in life exists! –
tip here the balance, which no scale can measure.

Beware the dog nearby with its hot lips,
and the criminal who is sated on raw blood,

sich volltrinkt, bis es Schatten übersetzen
in schwarzer Lachen herrenloses Gut.

Und einen Blutsturz später: Wangenflecken –
die erste Scham, weil Schmerz und Schuld bestehn
und Eingeweide ausgenommner Tiere
in Zeichen erster Zukunft übergehn;

weil süßem Fleisch und markgefüllten Knochen
ein Atem ausbleibt, wo der deine geht.
Den Ahnenrock am abgestellten Rocken
hat unversehens Spinnweb überweht.

Die Augen gehen über. Jahre sinken.
Die junge Braue fühlt den weißen Stift.
Und die Gerippe steigen aus dem Anger,
die Kreuze mit der dürren Blumenschrift.

VII

Zum Fest sind alle Seelen rein gewaschen,
der Bretterboden wird gelaugt vorm Tanz,
die Kinder hauchen gläubig in das Wasser,
am Halm erscheint der schöne Seifenglanz.

Der Maskenzug biegt um die Häuserzeile,
Strohpuppen torkeln an die Weizenwand,
die Reiter sprengen über Blumenbarren,
und die Musik zieht in das Sommerland.

Maultrommeln klagen zu den Flötenstimmen.
Die Axt der Nacht fällt in das morsche Licht.
Der Krüppel reicht den Buckel zum Befingern.
Der Idiot entdeckt sein Traumgesicht.

until the shadows eventually transform it
into standing black pools of ownerless goods.

And a spurt of blood later: the cheeks aflush –
the first felt shame, since pain and guilt exist;
what follows are the entrails, the animals' guts,
that as symbols spill into the future first;

meanwhile it's marrow bones and their sweet flesh
that breathe a breath, as you do yours, no longer.
On a spinning wheel that's stopped, a cobweb mesh
has stealthily covered the dress of an ancestor.

The eyes fill up with tears. Years sink away.
Young eyebrows feel the prick of white thorns.
The skeletons are climbing out of silent graves
past crosses that only withered flowers adorn.

VII

Made ready for celebration, all souls are cleansed,
as children blow faithfully into the water;
the floorboards are scrubbed down before the dance,
on blades of grass appears the dew's white lather.

The masquerade now winds around the houses,
scarecrows begin to wheel in fields of wheat,
as riders leap on horses over flowered trusses,
and music drifts over fields with summer's heat.

To the voices of the flutes, the Jew's harp laments.
The night's ax sinks into the decaying light.
So others can finger his hump, the cripple bends.
The idiot discovers the face he dreamt of last night.

Der Holzstoß flammt: die Werke und die Tage
holt er vorm Anlauf, vor dem neuen Mond;
die Samen und die Funken gehn zu Sternen,
und sie erfahren, was im Himmel lohnt.

Die Schüsse überfliegen Tannenzüge.
Ein Schuß fällt immer, der im Fleisch verhallt.
Und Einer bleibt am Ort, verscharrt in Nadeln
und stumm gemacht vom Moos im schwarzen Wald.

Zum Kehraus drängen traurige Gendarmen.
Die Füße stampfen einen wilden Reim,
und umgestimmt vom strömenden Wacholder
schwanken verloren die Betrunknen heim.

Im Dunkel flattern lange die Girlanden,
und das Papier treibt schaurig übers Dach.
Der Wind räumt auf in den verlassnen Buden
und trägt den Träumern Zuckerherzen nach.

VIII

(Hab ich sie nicht erfunden, diese Seen
und diesen Fluß! Und kennt noch wer den Berg?
Geht einer durch ein Land mit Riesenschritten,
verläßt sich einer auf den guten Zwerg?

Die Himmelsrichtung? Und die Wendekreise?
Du fragst noch?! Nimm dein feurigstes Gespann,
fahr diesen Erdball ab, roll mit den Tränen
die Welt entlang! Dort kommst du niemals an.

Was ruft uns, daß sich so die Haare sträuben?
Tollkirschen schwingen um das heiße Ohr.

The pile of wood burns: the gathered works and days
go up in smoke before the new moon ascends;
to the stars, the seeds and rising sparks float away,
and learn what just reward exists in the heavens.

Gunshots now fly above the forest of firs.
One shot always sinks within the thud of flesh.
And one stays buried where pine needles gather,
and by the black wood's moss is silently enmeshed.

By sad gendarmes the final dance is ordered.
The dancers' feet stomp out their own wild rhythms,
while, senses still aswim with the flowing liquor,
lost drunkards stagger slowly towards their homes.

Long into the night remain the fluttering garlands,
and above rooftops drift ghostly paper streamers.
The wind cleans out the abandoned market stands
and tumbles hearts of sugar back to the dreamers.

VIII

(Have I not invented them, these very lakes,
also this river! Who knows that mountain at a glance!
Through a land is it the giant's steps one takes?
Does anyone rely on the good dwarf's guidance?

This quadrant of the sky? And the latitudes?
You question me still? Harness your fieriest mare,
drive all around this globe, with tears roll through
the world! You'll never reach the destination there.

What cries to us, causing our hair to bristle?
Belladonna swings next to the feverish ear.

Die Adern lärmen, überfüllt von Stille.
Die Totenglocke schaukelt überm Tor.

Was kümmern uns die ländlich blinden Fenster,
das Lämmerzeug, der Schorf, das Altenteil?
Nach Unverwandtem trachten Mund und Augen.
Uns wird die bleibende Figur zuteil.

Was sind uns Pferde und die braunen Wolken,
Windwolf und Irrlicht, braver Hörnerschall!
Wir sind zu andren Zielen aufgestiegen,
und andre Hürden bringen uns zu Fall.

Was kümmern uns der Mond und was die Sterne,
uns, deren Stirnen dunkeln und erglühn!
Beim Untergang des schönsten aller Länder
sind wir's, die es als Traum nach innen ziehn.

Wo ist Gesetz, wo Ordnung? Wo erscheinen
uns ganz begreiflich Blatt und Baum und Stein?
Zugegen sind sie in der schönen Sprache,
im reinen Sein . . .)

IX

Es kommt der Bruder mit den Weißdornaugen,
den Hecken auf der Brust, dem Vogelleim;
die Amsel fliegt im Sturz auf seine Rute
und treibt mit ihm die Rinderherde heim.

In seinen blonden Haaren wird sie nisten,
im Stall, wenn er in Halmen untergeht,
den Tierdunst atmet, nach dem Schattenhalfter
und einem Rappen für den Sattel späht.

The veins beat loudly on, aflood with quiet.
The death bell tolls above the doorway here.

What's it to us, the blind and rustic window,
lamb's wool, the scaly skin, land sold to retire?
Towards what is other strive our eyes and mouth.
Our reference point remains the immortal figure.

What do horses mean to us, or even brown clouds,
hunting horns, greyhounds, or the will-o'-the-wisp!
It is towards other goals that we have climbed,
it's attempting quite other hurdles that we trip.

What is the moon to us, and what do stars mean,
to us, or to brows so dark and glowing bright!
At the downfall of the most beautiful of lands
we are what it absorbs, much like a dream at night.

Where is there law, where order? Where do we see
the wholly comprehensible leaf or tree or stone?
They are only present in language's beauty,
in Being's pure tone…)

IX

My brother is approaching with hawthorn eyes,
past hedgerows laced with birdlime at chest level;
landing upon his stick, the blackbird dives,
helping him drive home the herd of cattle.

In his blond hair it will later build its nest
when he collapses on straw inside the stable,
breathing in the fumes of the animal scents,
searching for a halter and a black horse's saddle.

Ins Rosenöl wird sie den Schnabel tunken,
in seine Augen tropft sie Rosenlicht.
Die Nacht steigt in ihr schwellendes Gefieder
und hebt sie auf im seligen Verzicht.

»O Schwester sing, so sing von fernen Tagen!«
»Bald sing ich, bald, an einem schönren Ort.«
»O sing und web den Teppich aus den Liedern
und flieg auf ihm mit mir noch heute fort!

Halt mit mir Rast, wo Bienen uns bewirten,
mich Engelschön im Engelhut besucht . . .«
»Bald sing ich – doch im Turm beginnt's zu schwirren,
schlaf ein! es ist die Zeit der Eulenflucht.«

Die Kürbisleuchter machen ihre Runde,
der Knecht springt auf, die Peitsche in der Hand,
er starrt ins Licht und überrascht die Amsel
am Ausgang in das letzte Hirtenland.

Die Sense ficht mit ihren wilden Flügeln,
die Gabel sticht die Flatternde ans Tor.
Doch eh den Schläfer ihre Schreie wecken,
erschrickt sein Herz im ersten Rosenflor.

X

Im Land der tiefen Seen und der Libellen,
den Mund erschöpft ans Urgestein gepreßt,
ruft einer nach dem Geist der ersten Helle,
eh er für immer dieses Land verläßt.

Im Schaumkraut badet er die wehen Augen;
kalt und entzaubert sieht er, was er sah.

It will dip its beak into the oil of roses,
and then into his eyes it will drip rose light.
Into its swollen plumage the night now rises,
the blackbird absorbing it, blessedly resigned.

"O sister sing, O sing of the days to come!"
"Soon I will sing; soon in a lovelier place."
"O sing and weave together the carpet of song,
and together on it today, come, let us race!

Then rest with me, where bees will entertain us,
myself an angelic beauty whom angels attend...."
"Soon I will sing — yet in the tower there rustles
a bird — so sleep, for the owl will soon ascend."

The jack-o-lanterns begin to make their rounds,
the farm boy jumps up from straw, a whip in hand,
he stares into the light as the blackbird bounds
from the gate into the distant pasture land.

The scythe now slices the air with its wild wings,
a pitchfork nails its fluttering to the stake.
Yet before the sleeper is awakened by its screams,
his heart, at dawn's first light, startles him awake.

X

In the land of deep lakes and the dragonflies,
having placed a tired kiss on the ancient stone,
he calls to the spirit of the morning's first light
before he leaves this land he called his own.

He bathes his weary eyes in the cardamine;
cold and disenchanted, he sees again what he saw.

Was unbesiegbar macht, wird ihm gegeben:
das weite Herz und die Harmonika.

Es ist die Zeit des Apfelmosts, der Schwalben;
den Fässern wird das Spundloch eingedrückt.
Wer jetzt trinkt, trinkt auf schwarze Vogelzüge,
und jede Ferne macht sein Herz verrückt.

Er schließt die Schmieden, Mühlen und Kapellen,
er geht durchs Maisfeld, schlägt die Kolben ab,
die Körner springen auf mit goldnen Funken,
und es erlischt schon, was ihm Nahrung gab.

Zum Abschied schwören die Geschwister
auf ihren Bund aus Schweigen und Vertraun.
Der Klettenkranz wird aus dem Haar gerissen,
und keines wagt, vom Boden aufzuschaun.

Die Vogelnester stürzen aus den Ästen,
der Zunder brennt, das Feuer wühlt im Laub,
und an den blauen Bienenstöcken rächen
die Engel den verjährten Honigraub.

O Engelstille, wenn im Gehn die Fäden
in alle Lüfte ausgeworfen sind!
Zu allem frei, wird sich die Hand nicht lösen,
die einen fängt vorm Gang ins Labyrinth.

What will keep him from harm, he will be given:
the ample, yearning heart and the harmonica.

It is the time of apple cider and swallows,
as all around the spigot pierces the cask.
Whoever drinks now toasts the birds flying south,
though distance maddens his heart because it's so vast.

He closes up the foundries, the mills and chapels;
he pulls off ears of corn as he walks through fields;
the corn heaps up in piles of golden sparkles,
which extinguish as they nourish, becoming his yield.

In leaving, the siblings vow to one another,
swearing a sacred silence to which they're bound.
A garland of burdocks is torn out from the hair,
as no one dares lift up his eyes from the ground.

Bird's nests outside fall down from the branches;
the tinder burns, the fire engulfs each leaf;
meanwhile, atop blue beehives the angels plan
to avenge, in ages past, the honey's thief.

O the peace of angels, when in passing, threads
haphazardly are scattered upon the winds!
Though free to move, the hand remains enmeshed,
which keeps one from entering the labyrinth.

Anrufung des Großen Bären

Großer Bär, komm herab, zottige Nacht,
Wolkenpelztier mit den alten Augen,
Sternenaugen,
durch das Dickicht brechen schimmernd
deine Pfoten mit den Krallen,
Sternenkrallen,
wachsam halten wir die Herden,
doch gebannt von dir, und mißtrauen
deinen müden Flanken und den scharfen
halbentblößten Zähnen,
alter Bär.

Ein Zapfen: eure Welt.
Ihr: die Schuppen dran.
Ich treib sie, roll sie
von den Tannen im Anfang
zu den Tannen am Ende,
schnaub sie an, prüf sie im Maul
und pack zu mit den Tatzen.

Fürchtet euch oder fürchtet euch nicht!
Zahlt in den Klingelbeutel und gebt
dem blinden Mann ein gutes Wort,
daß er den Bären an der Leine hält.
Und würzt die Lämmer gut.

's könnt sein, daß dieser Bär
sich losreißt, nicht mehr droht
und alle Zapfen jagt, die von den Tannen
gefallen sind, den großen, geflügelten,
die aus dem Paradiese stürzten.

Invocation of the Great Bear

Great Bear, shaggy night, come down.
Cloud-furred one with old eyes,
starry eyes,
glimmering you break through the brush
on your pads with claws,
starry claws,
while watchful we tend the flocks,
spellbound, mistrusting
your weary flanks and sharp
half-exposed teeth,
old Bear.

Your world: a fir cone.
You: the fir cone's scales.
I nudge them, roll them
from the fir in the beginning
to the fir in the end,
sniff them, give them a lick or two,
and bat them about with my paws.

Afraid or not afraid,
pay into the basket and give
the blind man a good word
so that he keeps the Bear on a leash.
And season the lambs well.

For it just might be that this Bear
will break loose, threaten no more,
and hunt all cones, those fallen
from firs, the great, the wingéd,
those that from Paradise plunged.

Mein Vogel

Was auch geschieht: die verheerte Welt
sinkt in die Dämmrung zurück,
einen Schlaftrunk halten ihr die Wälder bereit,
und vom Turm, den der Wächter verließ,
blicken ruhig und stet die Augen der Eule herab.

Was auch geschieht: du weißt deine Zeit,
mein Vogel, nimmst deinen Schleier
und fliegst durch den Nebel zu mir.

Wir äugen im Dunstkreis, den das Gelichter bewohnt.
Du folgst meinem Wink, stößt hinaus
und wirbelst Gefieder und Fell –

Mein eisgrauer Schultergenoß, meine Waffe,
mit jener Feder besteckt, meiner einzigen Waffe!
Mein einziger Schmuck: Schleier und Feder von dir.

Wenn auch im Nadeltanz unterm Baum
die Haut mir brennt
und der hüfthohe Strauch
mich mit würzigen Blättern versucht,
wenn meine Locke züngelt,
sich wiegt und nach Feuchte verzehrt,
stürzt mir der Sterne Schutt
doch genau auf das Haar.

Wenn ich vom Rauch behelmt
wieder weiß, was geschieht,
mein Vogel, mein Beistand des Nachts,
wenn ich befeuert bin in der Nacht,

My Bird

Whatever happens: the devastated world
sinks back into twilight,
the forest holds its night potion ready,
and from the tower, which the sentry deserted,
the owl's eyes gaze downward, steady and calm.

Whatever happens: you know your time,
my bird, you take your veil
and fly through the fog to me.

We peer through smoke which the riffraff inhabit.
You obey my sign, fly off
and whirl your plumage and down.

My hoary gray shoulder-mate, my weapon,
bedecked with a feather, my only weapon!
My only adornment: veil and feather from you.

Although the fir's dance of needles
singes my skin
and the hip-high bush
tempts me with fragrant leaves,
when my curls leap up,
sway and long for dampness,
stardust still tumbles
directly onto my hair.

When I, crowned with smoke,
know again, whatever happens,
my bird, my nightly accomplice,
when I am ablaze at night,

knistert's im dunklen Bestand,
und ich schlage den Funken aus mir.

Wenn ich befeuert bleib wie ich bin
und vom Feuer geliebt,
bis das Harz aus den Stämmen tritt,
auf die Wunden träufelt und warm
die Erde verspinnt,
(und wenn du mein Herz auch ausraubst des Nachts,
mein Vogel auf Glauben und mein Vogel auf Treu!)
rückt jene Warte ins Licht,
die du, besänftigt,
in herrlicher Ruhe erfliegst –
was auch geschieht.

a dark grove begins to crackle
and I strike the sparks from my body.

When I remain as I am, ablaze,
loved by the fire,
until the resin seeps from the stems,
drips onto the wounds and, warm,
spins down to the earth,
(and also when you rob my heart at night,
my bird of belief and my bird of trust!)
that watchtower moves into the light
to which you, calmly,
in splendid quiet fly –
whatever happens.

II

Landnahme

Ins Weideland kam ich,
als es schon Nacht war,
in den Wiesen die Narben witternd
und den Wind, eh er sich regte.
Die Liebe graste nicht mehr,
die Glocken waren verhallt
und die Büschel verhärmt.

Ein Horn stak im Land,
vom Leittier verrannt,
ins Dunkel gerammt.

Aus der Erde zog ich's,
zum Himmel hob ich's
mit ganzer Kraft.

Um dieses Land mit Klängen
ganz zu erfüllen,
stieß ich ins Horn,
willens im kommenden Wind
und unter den wehenden Halmen
jeder Herkunft zu leben!

II

Settlement

Into pasture land I came
just after night had fallen,
scenting the scars in the meadows
and the wind before it rose.
Love no longer grazed,
the bells had faded away
and the sheaves stood bent and ragged.

A horn had been stuck in the earth
stubbornly by the herd's leader,
rammed into the darkness.

I drew it from the earth,
I lifted it to the sky
with all my might.

Wanting to fill this land
completely with music,
I blew the horn,
resolved in the rising wind
to live among the swaying grasses
of every true origin!

Curriculum Vitae

Lang ist die Nacht,
lang für den Mann,
der nicht sterben kann, lang
unter Straßenlaternen schwankt
sein nacktes Aug und sein Aug
schnapsatemblind, und Geruch
von nassem Fleisch unter seinen Nägeln
betäubt ihn nicht immer, o Gott,
lang ist die Nacht.

Mein Haar wird nicht weiß,
denn ich kroch aus dem Schoß von Maschinen,
Rosenrot strich mir Teer auf die Stirn
und die Strähnen, man hatt' ihr
die schneeweiße Schwester erwürgt. Aber ich,
der Häuptling, schritt durch die Stadt
von zehnmalhunderttausend Seelen, und mein Fuß
trat auf die Seelenasseln unterm Lederhimmel,
      aus dem
zehnmalhunderttausend Friedenspfeifen
hingen, kalt. Engelsruhe
wünscht' ich mir oft
und Jagdgründe, voll
vom ohnmächtigen Geschrei
meiner Freunde.

Mit gespreizten Beinen und Flügeln,
binsenweis stieg die Jugend
über mich, über Jauche, über Jasmin ging's
in die riesigen Nächte mit dem Quadrat-
wurzelgeheimnis, es haucht die Sage
des Tods stündlich mein Fenster an,

Curriculum Vitae

Long is the night,
long for the man
who cannot die, long
the feel of his shifting naked eye
under street lamps, and his eye
blind drunk on schnapps, and the smell
of moist flesh under his nails
is the briefest of drugs, oh God,
long is the night.

My hair will not turn white
for I crawled out of the womb of machines,
Rose Red smeared tar on my forehead
and curls, someone had strangled
her snow-white sister. But I,
a captain, marched through the city
of ten hundred thousand souls, and my foot
lowered onto the scurrying soul-centipedes
a leather sky, from which ten hundred thousand
pipes of peace hung cold. Often I've wished
for the quiet of angels
and hunting grounds filled
with the powerless cries
of my friends.

With outspread legs and wings,
the young with their clichés
leap over me, over dung, over jasmine
with the square root of a secret
into the towering nights, the saga of death
breathing against my window each hour

Wolfsmilch gebt mir und schüttet
in meinen Rachen das Lachen
der Alten vor mir, wenn ich in Schlaf
fall über den Folianten,
in den beschämenden Traum,
daß ich nicht taug für Gedanken,
mit Troddeln spiel,
aus denen Schlangen fransen.

Auch unsere Mütter haben
von der Zukunft ihrer Männer geträumt,
sie haben sie mächtig gesehen,
revolutionär und einsam,
doch nach der Andacht im Garten
über das flammende Unkraut gebeugt,
Hand in Hand mit dem geschwätzigen
Kind ihrer Liebe. Mein trauriger Vater,
warum habt ihr damals geschwiegen
und nicht weitergedacht?

Verloren in den Feuerfontänen,
in einer Nacht neben einem Geschütz,
das nicht feuert, verdammt lang
ist die Nacht, unter dem Auswurf
des gelbsüchtigen Monds, seinem galligen
Licht, fegt in der Machttraumspur
über mich (das halt ich nicht ab)
der Schlitten mit der verbrämten
Geschichte hinweg.
Nicht daß ich schlief: wach war ich,
zwischen Eisskeletten sucht' ich den Weg,
kam heim, wand mir Efeu
um Arm und Bein und weißte
mit Sonnenresten die Ruinen.
Ich hielt die hohen Feiertage,

Give me spurge milk and pour
the laughter of the ancients
into my throat, as in sleep
I stumble over tomes
in the shameful dream
where I'm not worthy of knowledge,
where I'm twirling tassels
whose fringes are snakes.

Our mothers have also dreamed
of the future of their men,
seeing them as powerful,
revolutionary, and lonesome,
yet after prayers in the garden,
bent over the flaming weeds,
hand in hand with the babbling
child of their love. My sad father,
why then did you all stay silent
and think no farther?

Lost among flaming fountains,
in a night next to a cannon
that will not fire, damned long
is the night, as under the detritus
of the jaundiced moon, its bilious light,
a sled brocaded with history
sweeps over me (I cannot stop it),
rushing along the trail
left by the dream of power.
Not that I was sleeping: I was awake,
and seeking the path between ice skeletons,
I came home, wound the ivy
around my arm and leg, painting
the ruins white with the sun's remains.
I observed the holy days,

und erst wenn es gelobt war,
brach ich das Brot.

In einer großspurigen Zeit
muß man rasch von einem Licht
ins andre gehen, von einem Land
ins andre, unterm Regenbogen,
die Zirkelspitze im Herzen,
zum Radius genommen die Nacht.
Weit offen. Von den Bergen
sieht man Seen, in den Seen
Berge, und im Wolkengestühl
schaukeln die Glocken
der einen Welt. Wessen Welt
zu wissen, ist mir verboten.

An einem Freitag geschah's
– ich fastete um mein Leben,
die Luft troff vom Saft der Zitronen
und die Gräte stak mir im Gaumen –
da löst' ich aus dem entfalteten Fisch
einen Ring, der, ausgeworfen
bei meiner Geburt, in den Strom
der Nacht fiel und versank.
Ich warf ihn zurück in die Nacht.

O hätt ich nicht Todesfurcht!
Hätt ich das Wort,
(verfehlt ich's nicht),
hätt ich nicht Disteln im Herz,
(schlüg ich die Sonne aus),
hätt ich nicht Gier im Mund,
(tränk ich das wilde Wasser nicht),
schlüg ich die Wimper nicht auf,
(hätt ich die Schnur nicht gesehn).

and only when it was blessed
did I break the bread.

In an overbearing age
one must flee from one light
into another, from one land
into another, beneath the rainbow,
the compass points stuck in the heart
and night the radius.
Then the open view. From the mountains
one sees lakes, in the lakes,
mountains, and in the belfries of clouds
swing the bells of the one
and only world. To know
just whose world, this is forbidden to me.

It happened on a Friday
— I fasted for my life,
the air dripped with the juice of lemons,
and a fish bone stuck in my gums —
then out of the gutted fish I lifted
a ring that, tossed away
at my birth, had fallen into
the stream of night and sunk.
I threw it back into the night.

Oh if only I had no fear of death!
If I had the word
(I wouldn't misplace it),
if I had no thistles in my heart
(I would drink up the sun),
if I had no greed in my mouth
(I wouldn't drink the wild water),
if I didn't open my eyelids
(I wouldn't see the rope).

Ziehn sie den Himmel fort?
Trüg mich die Erde nicht,
läg ich schon lange still,
läg ich schon lang,
wo die Nacht mich will,
eh sie die Nüstern bläht
und ihren Huf hebt
zu neuen Schlägen,
immer zum Schlag.
Immer die Nacht.
Und kein Tag.

Are they dislodging the sky?
If the earth had not held me
I'd long be lying still.
I'd long be lying
where the night wants me,
before it rears up snorting
and lifts its hoof
to strike yet another blow,
always a blow.
Always the night.
And never day.

Heimweg

Nacht aus Schlüsselblumen
und verwunschnem Klee,
feuchte mir die Füße,
daß ich leichter geh.

Der Vampir im Rücken
übt den Kinderschritt,
und ich hör ihn atmen,
wenn er kreuzweis tritt.

Folgt er mir schon lange?
Hab ich wen gekränkt?
Was mich retten könnte,
ist noch nicht verschenkt.

Wo die Halme zelten
um den Felsenspund,
bricht es aus der Quelle
altem, klarem Mund:

»Um nicht zu verderben,
bleib nicht länger aus,
hör das Schlüsselklirren,
komm ins Wiesenhaus!

Reinen Fleischs wird sterben,
wer es nicht mehr liebt,
über Rausch und Trauer
nur mehr Nachricht gibt.«

The Way Home

In the night of cowslip
and bewitching clover,
I moisten my feet
so my step is lighter.

The vampire behind me
mimics my own stride,
and I hear him breathe
whenever he steps aside.

How long has he followed?
Have I offended someone?
A means for being rescued
has not yet been given.

Where the grasses ring
the edge of the rocky pool,
there rises from the spring
a voice ancient and cool:

"So as not to come to ruin
don't stay out much longer;
listen, the key is rattling,
run for the meadow's shelter.

As a body no longer cared for
will surely meet its end,
it's delirium and sorrow
we hear about more often."

Mit der Kraft des Übels,
das mich niederschlug,
weitet seine Schwinge
der Vampir im Flug,

hebt die tausend Köpfe,
Freund- und Feindgesicht,
vom Saturn beschattet,
der den Ring zerbricht.

Ist das Mal gerissen
in die Nackenhaut,
öffnen sich die Türen
grün und ohne Laut.

Und die Wiesenschwelle
glänzt von meinem Blut.
Deck mir, Nacht, die Augen
mit dem Narrenhut.

With the power so menacing
that knocked me to the ground,
the vampire spreads his wings,
and away he bounds,

lifting over a thousand
faces of friends and enemies
in the shadow of Saturn's bands
that smash to smithereens.

Should the mark of his bite
sink into your skin,
doors will open wide
that are soundless and green.

It's then the meadow's edge
glistens with my blood.
My eyes, O night, protect
beneath a fool's hood.

Nebelland

Im Winter ist meine Geliebte
unter den Tieren des Waldes.
Daß ich vor Morgen zurückmuß,
weiß die Füchsin und lacht.
Wie die Wolken erzittern! Und mir
auf den Schneekragen fällt
eine Lage von brüchigem Eis.

Im Winter ist meine Geliebte
ein Baum unter Bäumen und lädt
die glückverlassenen Krähen
ein in ihr schönes Geäst. Sie weiß,
daß der Wind, wenn es dämmert,
ihr starres, mit Reif besetztes
Abendkleid hebt und mich heimjagt.

Im Winter ist meine Geliebte
unter den Fischen und stumm.
Hörig den Wassern, die der Strich
ihrer Flossen von innen bewegt,
steh ich am Ufer und seh,
bis mich Schollen vertreiben,
wie sie taucht und sich wendet.

Und wieder vom Jagdruf des Vogels
getroffen, der seine Schwingen
über mir steift, stürz ich
auf offenem Feld: sie entfiedert
die Hühner und wirft mir ein weißes
Schlüsselbein zu. Ich nehm's um den Hals
und geh fort durch den bitteren Flaum.

Fog Land

In winter my lover
lives among the beasts of the forest.
The vixen knows I must return
by morning, and she laughs.
How the clouds tremble! On my
snow collar a shower
of brittle ice falls.

In winter my lover
is a tree among trees, inviting
the hapless crows to nest
in her beautiful limbs. She knows
that the wind, when dusk falls,
will lift her stiff, frost-covered
evening dress and chase me home.

In winter my lover
is a fish among fish and mute.
A slave to waters that her fins
stroke from within,
I stand on the bank and watch,
till ice floes drive me away,
how she dives and turns.

And hearing the bird's hunting call
as above me it arches
its wings, I fall
onto an open field: she plucks
the hens and tosses me a white
collar bone. I hang it around my neck
and walk off through the bitter down.

Treulos ist meine Geliebte,
ich weiß, sie schwebt manchmal
auf hohen Schuh'n nach der Stadt,
sie küßt in den Bars mit dem Strohhalm
die Gläser tief auf den Mund,
und es kommen ihr Worte für alle.
Doch diese Sprache verstehe ich nicht.

Nebelland hab ich gesehen,
Nebelherz hab ich gegessen.

Faithless is my lover,
for I know she sometimes slips off
on high heels to town,
kissing the glasses in bars
deep in the mouth with a straw,
finding a spare word for everyone.
But I don't understand this talk.

For it's fog land I have seen.
Fog heart I have eaten.

Die blaue Stunde

Der alte Mann sagt: mein Engel, wie du willst,
wenn du nur den offenen Abend stillst
und an meinem Arm eine Weile gehst,
den Wahrspruch verschworener Linden verstehst,
die Lampen, gedunsen, betreten im Blau,
letzte Gesichter! nur deins glänzt genau.
Tot die Bücher, entspannt die Pole der Welt,
was die dunkle Flut noch zusammenhält,
die Spange in deinem Haar, scheidet aus.
Ohne Aufenthalt Windzug in meinem Haus,
Mondpfiff – dann auf freier Strecke der Sprung,
die Liebe, geschleift von Erinnerung.

Der junge Mann fragt: und wirst du auch immer?
Schwör's bei den Schatten in meinem Zimmer,
und ist der Lindenspruch dunkel und wahr,
sag ihn her mit Blüten und öffne dein Haar
und den Puls der Nacht, die verströmen will!
Dann ein Mondsignal, und der Wind steht still.
Gesellig die Lampen im blauen Licht,
bis der Raum mit der vagen Stunde bricht,
unter sanften Bissen dein Mund einkehrt
bei meinem Mund, bis dich Schmerz belehrt:
lebendig das Wort, das die Welt gewinnt,
ausspielt und verliert, und Liebe beginnt.

Das Mädchen schweigt, bis die Spindel sich dreht.
Sterntaler fällt. Die Zeit in den Rosen vergeht: –
Ihr Herren, gebt mir das Schwert in die Hand,
und Jeanne d'Arc rettet das Vaterland.
Leute, wir bringen das Schiff durchs Eis,
ich halte den Kurs, den keiner mehr weiß.

The Blue Hour

The old man says: my angel, as you will,
it is the empty evening that you still,
when, with you upon my arm, together we go,
sharing the linden's secret, which only you know,
and streetlamps bloating, embarrassed in the blue,
the day's last faces! while only yours shines through.
The books shut, dead, the world free of its axis,
what holds the flood of dark in place still is
your hair's bright comb, till it as well falls out.
Without delay then, a draft puffs through my house,
a moon's low whistle – then on open tracks the churn
into love that, dragged from memory, at last returns.

The young man asks: you'll always love me most of all?
Swear it by the shadows upon my bedroom wall,
and should the linden's whisper be dark and true,
recite it with blossoms, and let your hair loose –
its pulse of night that so badly wants to spill!
Then a signal from the moon and the wind falls still.
In evening's blue light, the lamps seem intimate,
till space breaks through, its hours indeterminate,
as with soft nibbling lips your own mouth turns
to seek my own, until with pain you learn:
what wins the world is still a living word,
one played and already lost, before love is stirred.

The girl is silent until the spindle spins.
Coins fall from the sky. The time of roses ends.
You men, just pass the sword into my hand
and Joan of Arc will save the fatherland.
People, we'll sail the ship through icy floes,
for I know the course to take that no one knows.

Kauft Anemonen! drei Wünsche das Bund,
die schließen vorm Hauch eines Wunsches den Mund.
Vom hohen Trapez im Zirkuszelt
spring ich durch den Feuerreifen der Welt,
ich gebe mich in die Hand meines Herrn,
und er schickt mir gnädig den Abendstern.

Buy anemones! Three wishes to a bundle;
with every wish you breathe, they close each petal.
As from the circus tent's trapeze I swoop,
I spring clear through the world's own flaming hoop,
surrendering myself to the hands of my partner,
giving me, like a gentleman, the evening star.

Erklär mir, Liebe

Dein Hut lüftet sich leis, grüßt, schwebt im Wind,
dein unbedeckter Kopf hat's Wolken angetan,
dein Herz hat anderswo zu tun,
dein Mund verleibt sich neue Sprachen ein,
das Zittergras im Land nimmt überhand,
Sternblumen bläst der Sommer an und aus,
von Flocken blind erhebst du dein Gesicht,
du lachst und weinst und gehst an dir zugrund,
was soll dir noch geschehen –

Erklär mir, Liebe!

Der Pfau, in feierlichem Staunen, schlägt sein Rad,
die Taube stellt den Federkragen hoch,
vom Gurren überfüllt, dehnt sich die Luft,
der Entrich schreit, vom wilden Honig nimmt
das ganze Land, auch im gesetzten Park
hat jedes Beet ein goldner Staub umsäumt.

Der Fisch errötet, überholt den Schwarm
und stürzt durch Grotten ins Korallenbett.
Zur Silbersandmusik tanzt scheu der Skorpion.
Der Käfer riecht die Herrlichste von weit;
hätt ich nur seinen Sinn, ich fühlte auch,
daß Flügel unter ihrem Panzer schimmern,
und nähm den Weg zum fernen Erdbeerstrauch!

Erklär mir, Liebe!

Tell Me, Love

Your hat tips slightly, greets, sways in the wind,
your uncovered head has touched the clouds,
your heart is busy elsewhere,
your mouth takes on new tongues,
the quaking-grass is growing fast,
summer blows asters to and fro,
blinded by tufts you lift your face,
you laugh and cry and fall to pieces,
what will become of you —

Tell me, love!

The peacock spreads its tail in festive wonder,
the dove lifts high its feathered collar,
bursting with coos, the air expands,
the drake cries, the whole land eats
wild honey, while in the tranquil park
each flower bed is edged with golden dust.

The fish blushes, overtakes the school
and plunges through grottoes into the coral bed.
To silver sand music the scorpion shyly dances.
The beetle scents his mate from afar;
if only I had his sense, I'd also feel
wings shimmering beneath her armored shell,
and I'd take the path to distant strawberry patches!

Tell me, love!

Wasser weiß zu reden,
die Welle nimmt die Welle an der Hand,
im Weinberg schwillt die Traube, springt und fällt.
So arglos tritt die Schnecke aus dem Haus!

Ein Stein weiß einen andern zu erweichen!

Erklär mir, Liebe, was ich nicht erklären kann:
sollt ich die kurze schauerliche Zeit
nur mit Gedanken Umgang haben und allein
nichts Liebes kennen und nichts Liebes tun?
Muß einer denken? Wird er nicht vermißt?

Du sagst: es zählt ein andrer Geist auf ihn . . .
Erklär mir nichts. Ich seh den Salamander
durch jedes Feuer gehen.
Kein Schauer jagt ihn, und es schmerzt ihn nichts.

Water knows how to speak,
a wave takes a wave by the hand,
the grape swells in the vineyard, bursts and falls.
The guileless snail creeps out of his house.

One stone can soften another!

Tell me, love, what I cannot explain:
should I spend this brief, dreadful time
only with thoughts circulating and alone,
knowing no love and giving no love?
Must one think? Will one not be missed?

You say: another spirit is relying on him…
Tell me nothing. I watch the salamander
slip through every fire.
No dread haunts him, and he feels no pain.

Scherbenhügel

Vom Frost begattet die Gärten –
das Brot in den Öfen verbrannt –
der Kranz aus den Erntelegenden
ist Zunder in deiner Hand.

Verstumm! Verwahr deinen Bettel,
die Worte, von Tränen bestürzt,
unter dem Hügel aus Scherben,
der immer die Furchen schürzt.

Wenn alle Krüge zerspringen,
was bleibt von den Tränen im Krug?
Unten sind Spalten voll Feuer,
sind Flammenzungen am Zug.

Erschaffen werden noch Dämpfe
beim Wasser- und Feuerlaut.
O Aufgang der Wolken, der Worte,
dem Scherbenberg anvertraut!

Mound of Shards

Frost beds down the gardens –
in the oven the bread is burning –
the garland of harvest legends
in your hand is a piece of kindling.

Hush! Hide your pleading words,
stupefied by tears of sorrow,
beneath the mound of shards
that's always knotted the furrows.

When all the pitchers are smashed,
what's left of tears in the pitcher?
Below us are burning cracks,
and flaming tongues prevail there.

Steam will still be unfurled
in the hiss of water and fire.
Oh the ascent of clouds, of words,
entrusted to the shard pile's pyre!

Tage in Weiß

In diesen Tagen steh ich auf mit den Birken
und kämm mir das Weizenhaar aus der Stirn
vor einem Spiegel aus Eis.

Mit meinem Atem vermengt,
flockt die Milch.
So früh schäumt sie leicht.
Und wo ich die Scheibe behauch, erscheint,
von einem kindlichen Finger gemalt,
wieder dein Name: Unschuld!
Nach so langer Zeit.

In diesen Tagen schmerzt mich nicht,
daß ich vergessen kann
und mich erinnern muß.

Ich liebe. Bis zur Weißglut
lieb ich und danke mit englischen Grüßen.
Ich hab sie im Fluge erlernt.

In diesen Tagen denk ich des Albatros',
mit dem ich mich auf-
und herüberschwang
in ein unbeschriebenes Land.

Am Horizont ahne ich,
glanzvoll im Untergang,
meinen fabelhaften Kontinent
dort drüben, der mich entließ
im Totenhemd.

Ich lebe und höre von fern seinen Schwanengesang!

Days in White

These days I rise with the birches
and brush the corn hair from my brow
before a mirror of ice.

Blended with my breath,
milk is beaten.
This early it foams easily.
And where I fog the pane there appears,
traced by a child-like finger,
again your name: Innocence!
After all these years.

These days I feel no pain
that I can forget
or that I must remember.

I love. Incandescently
I love and give thanks with Ave Marias.
I learned them with ease.

These days I think of the albatross
with whom I swung
up and over
into an uncharted land.

On the horizon I ascertain,
splendid in the sunset,
my marvelous continent
just over there, releasing me
wrapped in a shroud.

I live, and from afar, I hear its swan song!

Harlem

Von allen Wolken lösen sich die Dauben,
der Regen wird durch jeden Schacht gesiebt,
der Regen springt von allen Feuerleitern
und klimpert auf dem Kasten voll Musik.

Die schwarze Stadt rollt ihre weißen Augen
und geht um jede Ecke aus der Welt.
Die Regenrhythmen unterwandert Schweigen.
Der Regenblues wird abgestellt.

Harlem

With barrel staves made loose by all the clouds,
the rain seeps out from every opened slit,
as rain from fire ladders leaps to the ground
and on a crate full of music drums its beat.

The ghetto rolls along with wide white eyes
and slips around each corner out of the world.
The rhythms of rain into the silence slide.
The blues of rain are no longer heard.

Reklame

Wohin aber gehen wir
ohne sorge sei ohne sorge
wenn es dunkel und wenn es kalt wird
sei ohne sorge
aber
mit musik
was sollen wir tun
heiter und mit musik
und denken
heiter
angesichts eines Endes
mit musik
und wohin tragen wir
am besten
unsre Fragen und den Schauer aller Jahre
in die Traumwäscherei ohne sorge sei ohne sorge
was aber geschieht
am besten
wenn Totenstille

eintritt

Advertisement

But where are we going
carefree be carefree
when it is dark and when it grows cold
be carefree
but
with music
what should we do
cheerful and with music
and think
cheerful
in facing the end
with music
and to where do we carry
best of all
our questions and dread of all the years
to the dream laundry carefree be carefree
but what happens
best of all
when dead silence

sets in

Toter Hafen

Feuchte Flaggen hängen an den Masten
in den Farben, die kein Land je trug,
und sie wehen für verschlammte Sterne
und den Mond, der grün im Mastkorb ruht.

Wasserwelt aus den Entdeckerzeiten!
Wellen überwuchern jeden Weg,
und von oben tropft das Licht aus Netzen
neuer Straßen, in die Luft verlegt.

Drunten blättern Wasser in den Bibeln,
und die Kompaßnadel steht auf Nacht.
Aus den Träumen wird das Gold gewaschen,
und dem Meer bleibt die Verlassenschaft.

Nicht ein Land, nicht eins blieb unbetreten!
Und zerrissen treibt das Seemannsgarn,
denn die tollen, lachenden Entdecker
fielen in den toten Wasserarm.

Dead Harbor

Damp flags hang upon the many masts,
colors that no country has ever flown;
under murky stars and a moon that rests
green within the lookout, they flutter on.

Watery world that explorers once traversed!
Waves obliterate each route they sailed,
as up above light trickles from the gridwork
of new flight paths, which on the air are laid.

Under the surface, water leafs through bibles,
and the compass needle is pointing straight at night.
Out of our dreams, gold can still be filtered,
while under the sea our legacy still lies.

Not one land, not one remained untrodden!
Yet we're still compelled by tattered sailor's yarns,
because of those explorers, laughing and wanton,
embraced, as they fell, by the channel's dead arm.

Rede und Nachrede

Komm nicht aus unsrem Mund,
Wort, das den Drachen sät.
's ist wahr, die Luft ist schwül,
vergoren und gesäuert schäumt das Licht,
und überm Sumpf hängt schwarz der Mückenflor.

Der Schierling bechert gern.
Ein Katzenfell liegt aus,
die Schlange faucht darauf,
der Skorpion tanzt an.

Dring nicht an unser Ohr,
Gerücht von andrer Schuld,
Wort, stirb im Sumpf,
aus dem der Tümpel quillt.

Wort, sei bei uns
von zärtlicher Geduld
und Ungeduld. Es muß dies Säen
ein Ende nehmen!

Dem Tier beikommen wird nicht, wer den Tierlaut
    nachahmt.
Wer seines Betts Geheimnis preisgibt, verwirkt sich alle
    Liebe.
Des Wortes Bastard dient dem Witz, um einen Törichten
    zu opfern.

Wer wünscht von dir ein Urteil über diesen Fremden?
Und fällst du's unverlangt, geh du von Nacht zu Nacht
mit seinen Schwären an den Füßen weiter, geh! komm
    nicht wieder.

Spoken and Rumored

Do not pass from of our mouth,
word, the one that's a dragon seed.
It's true, the air is muggy,
steeped and sour, the light foams,
and over the swamp floats a black cloud of mosquitoes.

The hemlock is fond of drinking.
A cat skin lies on display,
the snake hissing at it,
as the scorpion joins the party.

Do not press at our ears,
rumor of another's guilt;
word, die within the swamp
where the murky pool begins.

Word, remain for us
composed of tender patience
and impatience. This sowing
must come to an end!

The beast will not be caught by the one who mimics its call.
He who betrays the secret of his bed forfeits all love.
The word's bastard serves the joke, sacrificing a fool.

Who expects a judgement from you about this stranger?
And if you give it freely, walk then night after night
with his sores on your feet, walk on, and don't come back.

Wort, sei von uns,
freisinnig, deutlich, schön.
Gewiß muß es ein Ende nehmen,
sich vorzusehen.

(Der Krebs zieht sich zurück,
der Maulwurf schläft zu lang,
das weiche Wasser löst
den Kalk, der Steine spann.)

Komm, Gunst aus Laut und Hauch,
befestig diesen Mund,
wenn seine Schwachheit uns
entsetzt und hemmt.

Komm und versag dich nicht,
da wir im Streit mit soviel Übel stehen.
Eh Drachenblut den Widersacher schützt,
fällt diese Hand ins Feuer.
Mein Wort, errette mich!

Word, be that part of us
enlightened, clear, and beautiful.
Certainly an end must come,
so take it as warning.

(The crab skitters back,
the mole sleeps too long,
soft water loosens the stones
once embedded in the lime.)

Come, grace of sound and breath,
fortify this mouth,
even when its weakness
frightens and inhibits.

Come, and do not falter,
for we battle so much evil.
Rather than defend an enemy with dragon's blood,
this hand will fall into the fire.
Deliver me, my word!

Was wahr ist

Was wahr ist, streut nicht Sand in deine Augen,
was wahr ist, bitten Schlaf und Tod dir ab
als eingefleischt, von jedem Schmerz beraten,
was wahr ist, rückt den Stein von deinem Grab.

Was wahr ist, so entsunken, so verwaschen
in Keim und Blatt, im faulen Zungenbett
ein Jahr und noch ein Jahr und alle Jahre —
was wahr ist, schafft nicht Zeit, es macht sie wett.

Was wahr ist, zieht der Erde einen Scheitel,
kämmt Traum und Kranz und die Bestellung aus,
es schwillt sein Kamm und voll gerauften Früchten
schlägt es in dich und trinkt dich gänzlich aus.

Was wahr ist, unterbleibt nicht bis zum Raubzug,
bei dem es dir vielleicht ums Ganze geht.
Du bist sein Raub beim Aufbruch deiner Wunden;
nichts überfällt dich, was dich nicht verrät.

Es kommt der Mond mit den vergällten Krügen.
So trink dein Maß. Es sinkt die bittre Nacht.
Der Abschaum flockt den Tauben ins Gefieder,
wird nicht ein Zweig in Sicherheit gebracht.

Du haftest in der Welt, beschwert von Ketten,
doch treibt, was wahr ist, Sprünge in die Wand.
Du wachst und siehst im Dunkeln nach dem Rechten,
dem unbekannten Ausgang zugewandt.

What's True

What's true does not throw sand into your eyes;
what's true is that sleep and death want confirmation
from you within, as well as each pain's advice;
what's true, above your grave, will tip the stone.

What's true, so sunken in, so undefined
in a seed or leaf, and in lazy tongues embedded
for a year, another year, then for all time –
what's true does not buy time, it cancels it.

What's true can part the earth just like a comb
that rakes away dreams, commands, and laurel crowns,
till, full of plucked fruit, its proud and swollen comb
can set its teeth in you and strike you down.

What's true does not occur until the predator
attacks, thus causing you to stop at nothing.
That you're its prey your open wounds make clear;
though nothing wins that already hasn't won.

The moon is rising, and mugs full of regret.
So drink your fill. The night slides down so bitter.
The dove's own feathers will be covered by the dregs
if not a single branch is made secure.

You still cling to the world, burdened by chains,
and yet what's true still causes the wall to split.
You wake in darkness, note everything is the same,
aware there still exists an unknown exit.

III

Das erstgeborene Land

In mein erstgeborenes Land, in den Süden
zog ich und fand, nackt und verarmt
und bis zum Gürtel im Meer,
Stadt und Kastell.

Vom Staub in den Schlaf getreten
lag ich im Licht,
und vom ionischen Salz belaubt
hing ein Baumskelett über mir.

Da fiel kein Traum herab.

Da blüht kein Rosmarin,
kein Vogel frischt
sein Lied in Quellen auf.

In meinem erstgeborenen Land, im Süden
sprang die Viper mich an
und das Grausen im Licht.

O schließ
die Augen schließ!
Preß den Mund auf den Biß!

III

The Native Land

Into my native land, into the South,
I moved and found, naked and poor
and up to their waists in the sea,
a town and fortress.

Rising from dust into sleep,
I lay in the light,
and above hung a skeleton tree
covered with Ionian salt.

There no dream fell down.

There no rosemary blooms,
no bird renews
its song in spring waters.

In my native land, in the South,
the viper sprang at me
in that brutal light.

O shut
your eyes, shut them!
Press your mouth to the bite!

Und als ich mich selber trank
und mein erstgeborenes Land
die Erdbeben wiegten,
war ich zum Schauen erwacht.

Da fiel mir Leben zu.

Da ist der Stein nicht tot.
Der Docht schnellt auf,
wenn ihn ein Blick entzündet.

And when I drank of myself
and my native land
rocked with earthquakes,
I opened my eyes to see.

Then life fell to me.

There the stone is not dead.
The wick flares
when lit by a glance.

Lieder von einer Insel

Schattenfrüchte fallen von den Wänden,
Mondlicht tüncht das Haus, und Asche
erkalteter Krater trägt der Meerwind herein.

In den Umarmungen schöner Knaben
schlafen die Küsten,
dein Fleisch besinnt sich auf meins,
es war mir schon zugetan,
als sich die Schiffe
vom Land lösten und Kreuze
mit unsrer sterblichen Last
Mastendienst taten.

Nun sind die Richtstätten leer,
sie suchen und finden uns nicht.

———

Wenn du auferstehst,
wenn ich aufersteh,
ist kein Stein vor dem Tor,
liegt kein Boot auf dem Meer.

Morgen rollen die Fässer
sonntäglichen Wellen entgegen,
wir kommen auf gesalbten
Sohlen zum Strand, waschen
die Trauben und stampfen
die Ernte zu Wein,
morgen am Strand.

Wenn du auferstehst,
wenn ich aufersteh,

Songs from an Island

Ripe shadows cascade from the walls,
moonlight whitewashes the house, and ashes
from the cold crater drift on the sea breeze.

The surf sleeps in the embrace
of beautiful boys;
your flesh considers mine,
still as fond of me
as when the ships
broke loose from land,
and the crosses
with our mortal weight
kept watch as masts.

Now the gallows are empty,
they search but find us gone.

———————

When you rise again,
when I rise again,
no stone is before the gate,
no boat lies on the sea.

Tomorrow the barrels will roll
towards the Sunday waves.
We will walk the sand
on anointed soles, washing
the grapes and stomping
the harvest to wine,
tomorrow on the beach.

When you rise again,
when I rise again,

hängt der Henker am Tor,
sinkt der Hammer ins Meer.

————

Einmal muß das Fest ja kommen!
Heiliger Antonius, der du gelitten hast,
heiliger Leonhard, der du gelitten hast,
heiliger Vitus, der du gelitten hast.

Platz unsren Bitten, Platz den Betern,
Platz der Musik und der Freude!
Wir haben Einfalt gelernt,
wir singen im Chor der Zikaden,
wir essen und trinken,
die mageren Katzen
streichen um unseren Tisch,
bis die Abendmesse beginnt,
halt ich dich an der Hand
mit den Augen,
und ein ruhiges mutiges Herz
opfert dir seine Wünsche.

Honig und Nüsse den Kindern,
volle Netze den Fischern,
Fruchtbarkeit den Gärten,
Mond dem Vulkan, Mond dem Vulkan!

Unsre Funken setzten über die Grenzen,
über die Nacht schlugen Raketen
ein Rad, auf dunklen Flößen
entfernt sich die Prozession und räumt
der Vorwelt die Zeit ein,
den schleichenden Echsen,
der schlemmenden Pflanze,
dem fiebernden Fisch,

the hangman hangs on the gate,
the hammer sinks in the sea.

————

And yet the feast must come!
Holy Antonius, you who have suffered,
Holy Leonhard, you who have suffered,
Holy Vitus, you who have suffered.

Make way for our pleas, make way for the worshipers,
make way for music and joy!
We have learned a simpleness,
we sing in a chorus of cicadas,
we eat and drink,
while lean cats
rub against our table
until the evening mass begins,
and I hold your hand
with my eyes
and a quiet, courageous heart
offers you up its wishes.

Give honey and nuts to the children,
full nets to the fishermen,
fruitfulness to the gardens,
and a moon to the volcano! a moon to the volcano!

Our sparks crossed the borders,
above the night the rockets wheeled,
on dark rafts
the procession withdraws and yields
time to the prehistoric world,
to the creeping lizards,
gluttonous plants,
feverish fish,

den Orgien des Winds und der Lust
des Bergs, wo ein frommer
Stern sich verirrt, ihm auf die Brust
schlägt und zerstäubt.

Jetzt seid standhaft, törichte Heilige,
sagt dem Festland, daß die Krater nicht ruhn!
Heiliger Rochus, der du gelitten hast,
o der du gelitten hast, heiliger Franz.

———————

Wenn einer fortgeht, muß er den Hut
mit den Muscheln, die er sommerüber
gesammelt hat, ins Meer werfen
und fahren mit wehendem Haar,
er muß den Tisch, den er seiner Liebe
deckte, ins Meer stürzen,
er muß den Rest des Weins,
der im Glas blieb, ins Meer schütten,
er muß den Fischen sein Brot geben
und einen Tropfen Blut ins Meer mischen,
er muß sein Messer gut in die Wellen treiben
und seinen Schuh versenken,
Herz, Anker und Kreuz,
und fahren mit wehendem Haar!
Dann wird er wiederkommen.
Wann?
    Frag nicht.

———————

Es ist Feuer unter der Erde,
und das Feuer ist rein.

Es ist Feuer unter der Erde
und flüssiger Stein.

the wind's orgies
and the mountain's pleasure,
where a pious star strays and falls,
exploding upon the crest.

Now be steadfast, foolish saints,
tell the coast the craters are not resting!
Holy Rochus, you who have suffered,
O you who have suffered, Holy Franz.

———

When one goes away, he must fling
his hat of mussels gathered
over the summer into the sea
and sail with windblown hair.
He must plunge the table
set for his love into the sea.
He must pour the last of the wine
left in the glass into the sea.
He must feed the fish his bread
and mix a drop of blood into the sea.
He must throw his knife to the waves
and toss away his shoes,
heart, anchor, and cross,
and sail with windblown hair.
Only then will he return.
When?
   Don't ask.

———

There's a fire under the earth
and the fire burns clean.

There's a fire under the earth
and a molten stream.

Es ist ein Strom unter der Erde,
der strömt in uns ein.

Es ist ein Strom unter der Erde,
der sengt das Gebein.

Es kommt ein großes Feuer,
es kommt ein Strom über die Erde.

Wir werden Zeugen sein.

There's a stream under the earth
and we feel it in our souls.

There's a stream under the earth
and it singes our bones.

There will be a great fire.
There will be a great flood.

We shall witness each.

Nord und Süd

Zu spät erreichten wir der Gärten Garten
in jenem Schlaf, von dem kein dritter weiß.
Im Ölzweig wollte ich den Schnee erwarten,
im Mandelbaum den Regen und das Eis.

Wie aber soll die Palme es verwinden,
daß du den Wall aus warmen Lauben schleifst,
wie soll ihr Blatt sich in den Nebel finden,
wenn du die Wetterkleider überstreifst?

Bedenk, der Regen machte dich befangen,
als ich den offnen Fächer zu dir trug.
Du schlugst ihn zu. Dir ist die Zeit entgangen,
seit ich mich aufhob mit dem Vogelzug.

North and South

Too late we reached within our private sleep
the garden of gardens that no third can know.
I'd hoped to find within the almond tree
both rain and ice, and on olive branches, snow.

But how will the palm survive it when you raze
whole mounds of warm leaves, making them scatter,
or find its own leaf in the fog's thick haze
when you impose on it your coat of weather.

Remember how much the rain disturbed you
when I offered you the palm, its open fan.
Then you knocked it away. Its season left you
as soon as, with the birds, I fled your land.

Brief in zwei Fassungen

Rom im November abends besten Dank
das glatte Marmorriff die kalten Fliesen
die Gischt der Lichter eh die Tore schließen
der Klang mit dem erfrorne Gläser springen
der Singsang den sie aus Gitarren wringen
eh sie die Schädel in die Münzen stanzen
auf die Arena mit Zypressenlanzen!
der Holzwurm ist bei mir zu Tisch gesessen —
wie wohl ein Blatt aussieht das Raupen fressen?
und Herbst in Nebelland die bunten Lumpen
der Wälder unter großen Regenpumpen
ob es die Käuzchen gibt das Todeswerben
die Drachen die in warmen Sümpfen sterben
das Segel schwarz den Unglücksschrei der Raben
den Nordwind um die Wasser umzugraben
das Geisterschiff die Halden und die Heiden
schuttüberhäuft das Haus die Trauerweiden
verschuldet und vertränt am Strom aus Särgen
den Wahnsinn den sie aus der Tiefe bergen
Immer und Nimmermehr gemischt zum Trank
dein wehes Herz vergötternd alle Leiden
vernichtet und verloren liebeskrank . . .

Nachts im November Rom Einklang und Ruh
der Abschied ohne Kränkung ist vollzogen
die Augen hat ein reiner Glanz beflogen
die Säulen wachsen aus den Tamarinden
o Himmel den die blauen Töne binden!
es landen Disken in den Brunnenmitten
sie drehen sich zu leichten Rosenschritten
wollüstig dehnen Katzen ihre Krallen
der Schlaf hat einen letzten Stern befallen

Letter in Two Drafts

Rome in November evening many thanks
the smooth marble reef the cold tile-faces
the spray of lights before the gate closes
the sound that frozen glasses make when shattering
the singsong tune that from guitars keeps wringing
before it's more heads that into coins they press
down at the coliseum with lances of cypress!
the woodworm sits beside me at the table –
how juicy a leaf looks that caterpillars nibble?
and autumn in a land of fog the gaudy tatters
of forests that are soaked by great rain showers
whether it be a screech owl's longing for death
the dragons that in the marsh's warmth perish
the blackened sail the ominous call of ravens
the north wind over the water deviating
the ghostly ship the hillsides and the meadows
buried under rubble the house the willows
penniless and weeping at the stream of coffins
it's madness from the depths they keep recovering
Forever and No More mixed as a single drink
your pained heart glorifying every sorrow
destroyed completely lost lovesick you sink...

Roman nights in November harmonious and quiet
the goodbye without insult has been accomplished
the eyes by a pure luminescence have been brushed
the columns shoot up out of tamarinds
Oh the sky through which the blue tones wind!
petals are landing in the middle of fountains
like light rose-steps they continue turning
sensuously the cats stretch out their claws
sleep has seized hold of a last falling star

der Mund entkommt den Küssen ohne Kerben
der Seidenschuh ist unverletzt von Scherben
rasch sinkt der Wein durch dämmernde Gedanken
springt wieder Licht mit seinen hellen Pranken
umgreift die Zeiten schleudert sie ins Heute
die Hügel stürmt die erste Automeute
vor Tempeln paradieren die Antennen
empfangen Morgenchöre und entbrennen
für jeden Marktschrei Preise Vogelrufe
ins Pflaster taucht die Spiegelschrift der Hufe
die Chrysanthemen schütten Gräber zu
Meerhauch und Bergwind mischen Duft und Tränen
ich bin inmitten – was erwartest du?

the mouth escapes any kisses without a scratch
the silken slipper is not harmed by glass
the wine sinks fast through fading twilight thoughts
the light leaps up once more with its bright claws
embraces ages past flings them into today
up hillsides roar the hordes of cars at bay
around the temples antennas are parading
receiving morning's chorus amid the blazing
for every market cry of prices birds calling
into pavement horse hooves dip their mirror writing
chrysanthemums are what fill up the graves instead
sea breeze and mountain wind mix aromas and tears
I'm in the midst of it – what do you expect?

Römisches Nachtbild

Wenn das Schaukelbrett die sieben Hügel
nach oben entführt, gleitet es auch,
von uns beschwert und umschlungen,
ins finstere Wasser,

taucht in den Flußschlamm, bis in unsrem Schoß
die Fische sich sammeln.
Ist die Reihe an uns,
stoßen wir ab.

Es sinken die Hügel,
wir steigen und teilen
jeden Fisch mit der Nacht.

Keiner springt ab.
So gewiß ist's, daß nur die Liebe
und einer den andern erhöht.

Rome at Night

When the swing seat carries off
the seven hills, it also glides,
burdened and embraced by us,
into dark water,

diving into river mud, till in our lap
the fish gather.
Then when it's our turn
we cast off.

The hills sink away,
we climb and share
each fish with the night.

No one jumps off.
Proving that only by the love
of one is another lifted.

Unter dem Weinstock

Unter dem Weinstock im Traubenlicht
reift dein letztes Gesicht.
Die Nacht muß das Blatt wenden.

Die Nacht muß das Blatt wenden,
wenn die Schale zerspringt
und aus dem Fruchtfleisch die Sonne dringt.

Die Nacht muß das Blatt wenden,
denn dein erstes Gesicht
steigt in dein Trugbild, gedämmt vom Licht.

Unter dem Weinstock im Traubenstrahl
prägt der Rausch dir ein Mal –
Die Nacht muß das Blatt wenden!

Under the Grapevine

Under the grapevine in the light of grapes
there ripens your last face.
The night must turn over the leaf.

The night must turn over the leaf
when the peel bursts open
and out of the pulp there presses the sun.

The night must turn over the leaf
because your first face
is now a phantom held by light that fades.

Under the grapevine within the grapes' luster
delirium stamps you with its cipher –
The night must turn over leaf!

In Apulien

Unter den Olivenbäumen schüttet Licht die Samen aus,
Mohn erscheint und flackert wieder,
fängt das Öl und brennt es nieder,
und das Licht geht nie mehr aus.

Trommeln in den Höhlenstädten trommeln ohne Unterlaß,
weißes Brot und schwarze Lippen,
Kinder in den Futterkrippen
will der Fliegenschwarm zum Fraß.

Käm die Helle von den Feldern in den Troglodytentag,
könnt der Mohn aus Lampen rauchen,
Schmerz im Schlaf ihn ganz verbrauchen,
bis er nicht mehr brennen mag.

Esel stünden auf und trügen Wasserschläuche übers Land,
Schnüre stickten alle Hände,
Glas und Perlen für die Wände –
Tür im klingenden Gewand.

Die Madonnen stillten Kinder und der Büffel ging' vorbei,
Rauch im Horn, zur grünen Tränke,
endlich reichten die Geschenke:
Lammblut, Fisch und Schlangenei.

Endlich malmen Steine Früchte, und die Krüge sind
      gebrannt.
Öl rinnt offnen Augs herunter,
und der Mohn geht trunken unter,
von Taranteln überrannt.

In Apulia

Under the olive trees the light pours out its seeds,
poppies appear and begin to flicker,
burning the oil that feeds their fire;
it's a light that never recedes.

Drums inside cavernous cities drum their endless beat;
white bread and the lips still blackened,
manger cribs that are filled with children,
these attract the flies that feed.

If the light of fields revealed the prehistoric,
poppies would smoke inside the lanterns,
pain would consume their sleeping forms,
till its burning was exhausted.

Donkeys would rise to carry water over the land,
hands would embroider lacy curls,
adorning the walls with glass and pearls –
passages for the tinkling of raiment.

Children are nursed by madonnas, and the buffalo roam
munching green grass, smoke in their horns;
finally worthy gifts are borne:
snake eggs, fish, blood of the lamb.

Finally the stones crush fruit, the waiting jugs are fired.
Oil drops float like eyes on water,
poppies sink, drunken, as they falter,
overrun by deadly spiders.

Schwarzer Walzer

Das Ruder setzt auf den Gong mit dem schwarzen
   Walzer ein,
Schatten mit stumpfen Stichen nähn die Gitarren ein.

Unter der Schwelle erglänzt im Spiegel mein finsteres Haus,
Leuchter treten sich sanft die flammenden Spitzen aus.

Über die Klänge verhängt: Eintracht von Welle und Spiel;
immer entzieht sich der Grund mit einem anderen Ziel.

Schuld ich dem Tag den Marktschrei und den blauen
   Ballon –
Steinrumpf und Vogelschwinge suchen die Position

zum Pas de deux ihrer Nächte, lautlos mir zugewandt,
Venedig, gepfählt und geflügelt, Abend- und Morgenland!

Nur Mosaiken wurzeln und halten im Boden fest,
Säulen umtanzen die Bojen, Fratzen- und Freskenrest.

Kein August war geschaffen, die Löwensonne zu sehn,
schon am Eingang des Sommers ließ sie die Mähne wehn.

Denk dir abgöttische Helle, den Prankenschlag auf den Bug
und im Gefolge des Kiels den törichten Maskenzug,

überm ersäuften Parkett zu Spitze geschifft ein Tuch,
brackiges Wasser, die Liebe und ihren Geruch,

Introduktion, dann den Auftakt zur Stille und nichts
   nachher,
Pausen schlagende Ruder und die Coda vom Meer!

Black Waltz

The oar dips at the sound of a gong, the black waltz starts,
with thick dull stitches, shadows fall upon guitars.

Beneath the threshold, in a mirror, my dark house floats,
the flaring points of light now softly radiate out.

Hanging above the sounds: the harmony of waves in motion,
always the surface shifts towards another destination.

I owe the day its market cries and blue balloon —
stone torsos, the whirling flight of birds, the *pas de deux*

that they perform each night, silently turned towards me,
Venice, on pylons and floating, East and West in harmony!

Only mosaics strike roots and hold fast to the ground,
about a buoy — pillars, frescoes, and grimaces spin around.

There never was an August that saw the lion's sun,
for its mane was set adrift when the summer had begun.

Consider idolatrous light, the claw marks on the bow,
and in the wake of the keel, the carnival masks in tow,

as over the flooded plaza, to the tower, sails a garment,
also the brackish water, as well as love and its scent,

the introduction, a prelude to stillness, not another beat,
the oar that's striking intervals and the coda of the sea!

Nach vielen Jahren

Leicht ruht der Pfeil der Zeit im Sonnenbogen.
Wenn die Agave aus dem Felsen tritt,
wird über ihr dein Herz im Wind gewogen
und hält mit jedem Ziel der Stunde Schritt.

Schon überfliegt ein Schatten die Azoren
und deine Brust der zitternde Granat.
Ist auch der Tod dem Augenblick verschworen,
bist du die Scheibe, die ihm blendend naht.

Ist auch das Meer verwöhnt und glanzerfahren,
erhöht's den Spiegel für die Handvoll Blut,
und die Agave blüht nach vielen Jahren
im Schutz der Felsen vor der trunknen Flut.

After Many Years

Time's arrow easily rests in the sun's drawn bow.
As soon as the agave blossoms from the cliffs,
your heart will sway above in the wind that blows
with each hour's end, in step with its every tick.

Already a shadow drifts above the Azores
and over your breast's own trembling garnet.
Death is also the moment's conspirator,
and you, towards whom it streaks, the target.

The sea is also spoiled and vain, a mere
shift of its mirror swallowing a handful of blood,
just as the agave blooms after many years
in the shelter of cliffs, before the drunken flood.

Schatten Rosen Schatten

Unter einem fremden Himmel
Schatten Rosen
Schatten
auf einer fremden Erde
zwischen Rosen und Schatten
in einem fremden Wasser
mein Schatten

Shadows Roses Shadow

Under an alien sky
shadows roses
shadow
on an alien earth
between roses and shadows
in alien waters
my shadow

Bleib

Die Fahrten gehn zu Ende,
der Fahrtenwind bleibt aus.
Es fällt dir in die Hände
ein leichtes Kartenhaus.

Die Karten sind bebildert
und zeigen jeden Ort.
Du hast die Welt geschildert
und mischst sie mit dem Wort.

Profundum der Partien,
die dann im Gange sind!
Bleib, um das Blatt zu ziehen,
mit dem man sie gewinnt.

Stay

Now the journey is ending,
the wind is losing heart.
Into your hands it's falling,
a rickety house of cards.

The cards are backed with pictures
displaying all the world.
You've stacked up all the images
and shuffled them with words.

And how profound the playing
that once again begins!
Stay, the card you're drawing
is the only world you'll win.

Am Akragas

Das geklärte Wasser in den Händen,
an dem Mittag mit den weißen Brauen,
wird der Fluß die eigne Tiefe schauen
und zum letzten Mal die Dünen wenden,
mit geklärtem Wasser in den Händen.

Trägt der Wind aus Eukalyptushainen
Blätter hochgestrichen, hauchbeschrieben,
wird der Fluß die tiefren Töne lieben.
Festen Anschlag von den Feuersteinen
trägt der Wind zu Eukalyptushainen.

Und geweiht vom Licht und stummen Bränden
hält das Meer den alten Tempel offen,
wenn der Fluß, bis an den Quell getroffen,
mit geklärtem Wasser in den Händen
seine Weihen nimmt von stummen Bränden.

At Agrigento

The purified water held within its hands,
at midday, under the eyebrows of its white caps,
the river gazes deep into its depths,
winding its final stage through dunes of sand
with purified water held within its hands.

As from the eucalyptus groves, the wind
lifts leaves that carry the finest trace of dust,
the river begins to love the sea's deep thrust.
The readiness of sparks to be struck from flints
is carried to the eucalyptus groves by the wind.

Consecrated by light from silent fiery brands,
the sea still holds the ancient temple open,
as the river, returning to its origin,
with purified water held within its hands,
takes consecration from the silent fiery brands.

An die Sonne

Schöner als der beachtliche Mond und sein geadeltes Licht,
Schöner als die Sterne, die berühmten Orden der Nacht,
Viel schöner als der feurige Auftritt eines Kometen
Und zu weit Schönrem berufen als jedes andre Gestirn,
Weil dein und mein Leben jeden Tag an ihr hängt, ist die
    Sonne.

Schöne Sonne, die aufgeht, ihr Werk nicht vergessen hat
Und beendet, am schönsten im Sommer, wenn ein Tag
An den Küsten verdampft und ohne Kraft gespiegelt die
    Segel
Über dein Aug ziehn, bis du müde wirst und das letzte
    verkürzt.

Ohne die Sonne nimmt auch die Kunst wieder den
    Schleier,
Du erscheinst mir nicht mehr, und die See und der Sand,
Von Schatten gepeitscht, fliehen unter mein Lid.

Schönes Licht, das uns warm hält, bewahrt und wunderbar
    sorgt,
Daß ich wieder sehe und daß ich dich wiederseh!

Nichts Schönres unter der Sonne als unter der Sonne zu
    sein . . .

Nichts Schönres als den Stab im Wasser zu sehn und den
    Vogel oben,
Der seinen Flug überlegt, und unten die Fische im
    Schwarm,

To the Sun

More beautiful than the remarkable moon and its noble light,
More beautiful than the stars, the celebrated orders of night,
Much more beautiful than the fiery display of a comet,
And so much more beautiful than any planet,
Because your life and my life depend on it daily, is the sun.

Beautiful sun, which rises, remembering its tasks
And completing them, most beautiful in summer, when a day
Shimmers on the coast and the calm mirror of sails
Passes before your eye, until you tire and eventually doze.

Without the sun, even art puts on a veil again.
You cease to appear to me, and the sea and the sand,
Lashed by shadows, hide beneath my lids.

Beautiful light, which keeps us warm, sustains and marvelously
   ensures
That I see again, and that I see you again!

Nothing more beautiful under the sun than to be under the
   sun...

Nothing more beautiful than to see the reed in the water
   and the bird above
Pondering its flight and, below, the fish in their school,

Gefärbt, geformt, in die Welt gekommen mit einer
  Sendung von Licht,
Und den Umkreis zu sehn, das Geviert eines Felds, das
  Tausendeck meines Lands
Und das Kleid, das du angetan hast. Und dein Kleid,
  glockig und blau!

Schönes Blau, in dem die Pfauen spazieren und sich
  verneigen,
Blau der Fernen, der Zonen des Glücks mit den Wettern
  für mein Gefühl,
Blauer Zufall am Horizont! Und meine begeisterten Augen
Weiten sich wieder und blinken und brennen sich wund.

Schöne Sonne, der vom Staub noch die größte Bewundrung
  gebührt,
Drum werde ich nicht wegen dem Mond und den Sternen
  und nicht,
Weil die Nacht mit Kometen prahlt und in mir einen
  Narren sucht,
Sondern deinetwegen und bald endlos und wie um
  nichts sonst
Klage führen über den unabwendbaren Verlust
  meiner Augen.

Colorful, shapely, come into the world on a beam of light,
And to see the circumference, the square of a field, the
thousand corners of my land,
And the dress you have put on. Your dress, bell-shaped
and blue!

A beautiful blue in which peacocks strut and bow,
The blue of distances, zones of joy with climates for my
every mood,
The horizon's blue chance! And my enchanted eyes
Widen again and blink and burn themselves sore.

Beautiful sun, which even from dust deserves the highest
praise,
Causing me to raise a cry, not to the moon,
The stars, the night's garish comets that name me a fool,
But rather to you, and ultimately to you alone,
As I lament the inevitable loss of my sight.

IV

Lieder auf der Flucht

Dura legge d'Amor! ma, ben che obliqua,
Servar convensi; però ch'ella aggiunge
Di cielo in terra, universale, antiqua.
                    Petrarca, ›I Trionfi‹

I

Der Palmzweig bricht im Schnee,
die Stiegen stürzen ein,
die Stadt liegt steif und glänzt
im fremden Winterschein.

Die Kinder schreien und ziehn
den Hungerberg hinan,
sie essen vom weißen Mehl
und beten den Himmel an.

Der reiche Winterflitter,
das Mandarinengold,
treibt in den wilden Böen.
Die Blutorange rollt.

IV

Songs in Flight

Dura legge d'Amor! ma, ben che obliqua,
Servar convensi; però ch'ella aggiunge
Di cielo in terra, universale, antiqua.
                    Petrarch, I Trionfi

I

The palm branch breaks in snow
that collapses the stairway's flight,
the city lies stiff and gleaming
in a strange winter light.

The children wail and climb
their mountain of hunger,
praying to the sky
while they eat white flour.

Winter's wealth of tinsel
in a mandarin's gold,
the wind gusts wildly on,
and the blood orange rolls.

II

Ich aber liege allein
im Eisverhau voller Wunden.

Es hat mir der Schnee
noch nicht die Augen verbunden.

Die Toten, an mich gepreßt,
schweigen in allen Zungen.

Niemand liebt mich und hat
für mich eine Lampe geschwungen!

III

Die Sporaden, die Inseln,
das schöne Stückwerk im Meer,
umschwommen von kalten Strömen,
neigen noch Früchte her.

Die weißen Retter, die Schiffe
– o einsame Segelhand! –
deuten, eh sie versinken,
zurück auf das Land.

IV

Kälte wie noch nie ist eingedrungen.
Fliegende Kommandos kamen über das Meer.
Mit allen Lichtern hat der Golf sich ergeben.
Die Stadt ist gefallen.

II

But I lie alone,
wounds fill an abatis of ice.

The snow upon me
has yet to seal my eyes.

The dead press against me,
silent, no matter the tongue.

No one loves me,
no lamp for me is hung.

III

The Sporades, the islands,
patchwork in a sea so clear,
cold, the streams that surround them,
yet they bear the fruit that's here.

White rescuers, the ships,
– oh lonesome sailor's hand! –
they point, before they sink,
back towards the land.

IV

Cold, as never before, has penetrated.
Over the sea, commandos racing.
Down to its last lights, the bay has surrendered.
The city has fallen.

Ich bin unschuldig und gefangen
im unterwo fenen Neapel,
wo der Winter
Posilip und Vomero an den Himmel stellt,
wo seine weißen Blitze aufräumen
unter den Liedern
und er seine heiseren Donner
ins Recht setzt.

Ich bin unschuldig, und bis Camaldoli
rühren die Pinien die Wolken;
und ohne Trost, denn die Palmen
schuppt sobald nicht der Regen;

ohne Hoffnung, denn ich soll nicht entkommen,
auch wenn der Fisch die Flossen schützend sträubt
und wenn am Winterstrand der Dunst,
von immer warmen Wellen aufgeworfen,
mir eine Mauer macht,
auch wenn die Wogen
fliehend
den Fliehenden
dem nächsten Ziel entheben.

V

Fort mit dem Schnee von der gewürzten Stadt!
Der Früchte Luft muß durch die Straßen gehen.
Streut die Korinthen aus,
die Feigen bringt, die Kapern!
Belebt den Sommer neu,
den Kreislauf neu,
Geburt, Blut, Kot und Auswurf,
Tod – hakt in die Striemen ein,

I am guiltless and captive
in conquered Naples,
where winter
silhouettes Posilipo and Vomero,
where its white lightning cleans up
among the songs
and sets its hoarse thunder
in command.

I am guiltless, and until Camaldoli
stone pines nudge the clouds;
without comfort, because the rain
does not strip the palms;

without hope, because I shall not escape,
even though the fish bristles its fins
and the beach's winter mist
blown warm from the waves
protects and walls me in,
even though the tide
in fleeing
draws away the next goal
of those who flee.

V

Away with snow from the city fragrant with spice!
The scent of fruits must drift through the streets.
Scatter the currants,
bring the figs and the capers!
Renew the summer,
renew the cycle,
birth, blood, filth and scum,
death — sink into the welts,

die Linien auferlegt
Gesichtern
mißtrauisch, faul und alt,
von Kalk umrissen und in Öl getränkt,
von Händeln schlau,
mit der Gefahr vertraut,
dem Zorn des Lavagotts,
dem Engel Rauch
und der verdammten Glut!

VI

Unterrichtet in der Liebe
durch zehntausend Bücher,
belehrt durch die Weitergabe
wenig veränderbarer Gesten
und törichter Schwüre –

eingeweiht in die Liebe
aber erst hier –
als die Lava herabfuhr
und ihr Hauch uns traf
am Fuß des Berges,
als zuletzt der erschöpfte Krater
den Schlüssel preisgab
für diese verschlossenen Körper –

Wir traten ein in verwunschene Räume
und leuchteten das Dunkel aus
mit den Fingerspitzen.

deepen the lines
on faces
mistrustful, lazy and old,
engraved with chalk and drenched in oil,
sly from clever deals,
familiar with danger,
the anger of the lava god,
the smoke of angels
and the fire's cursed aura!

VI

Lessons in love
from ten thousand books,
taught in the sharing
of barely variable gestures
and foolish oaths –

initiated into love
but first knowing it here –
when the lava spilled over
and its breath reached us
at the foot of the mountain,
when finally the spent crater
surrendered the key
to these locked bodies –

We entered enchanted rooms
and illuminated the dark
with our fingertips.

VII

Innen sind deine Augen Fenster
auf ein Land, in dem ich in Klarheit stehe.

Innen ist deine Brust ein Meer,
das mich auf den Grund zieht.
Innen ist deine Hüfte ein Landungssteg
für meine Schiffe, die heimkommen
von zu großen Fahrten.

Das Glück wirkt ein Silbertau,
an dem ich befestigt liege.

Innen ist dein Mund ein flaumiges Nest
für meine flügge werdende Zunge.
Innen ist dein Fleisch melonenlicht,
süß und genießbar ohne Ende.
Innen sind deine Adern ruhig
und ganz mit dem Gold gefüllt,
das ich mit meinen Tränen wasche
und das mich einmal aufwiegen wird.

Du empfängst Titel, deine Arme umfangen Güter,
die an dich zuerst vergeben werden.

Innen sind deine Füße nie unterwegs,
sondern schon angekommen in meinen Samtlanden.
Innen sind deine Knochen helle Flöten,
aus denen ich Töne zaubern kann,
die auch den Tod bestricken werden . . .

VII

Within, your eyes are windows
to a land where in clarity I stand.

Within, your breast is a sea
that draws me to its bed.
Within, your hips are a quay
that greets my ships returning
from journeys too far from home.

Fortune weaves a silver chain
to which I lie attached.

Within, your mouth is a downy nest
for my fledgling, nascent tongue.
Within, your flesh is an endless light
sweet and ripe as a melon.
Within, your veins contain a quiet
wholly filled with the gold
that I wash with my tears,
and that one day will outweigh me.

Receiving your title, your arms embrace the goods,
which you are the first to be granted.

Within, your feet never wander,
but are already in my velvet land.
Within, your bones are bright flutes
on which I can conjure the tunes
that would even charm the dead…

VIII

. . . Erde, Meer und Himmel.
Von Küssen zerwühlt
die Erde,
das Meer und der Himmel.
Von meinen Worten umklammert
die Erde,
von meinem letzten Wort noch umklammert
das Meer und der Himmel!

Heimgesucht von meinen Lauten
diese Erde,
die schluchzend in meinen Zähnen
vor Anker ging
mit allen ihren Hochöfen, Türmen
und hochmütigen Gipfeln,

diese geschlagene Erde,
die vor mir ihre Schluchten entblößte,
ihre Steppen, Wüsten und Tundren,

diese rastlose Erde
mit ihren zuckenden Magnetfeldern,
die sich hier selbst fesselte
mit ihr noch unbekannten Kraftketten,

diese betäubte und betäubende Erde
mit Nachtschattengewächsen,
bleiernen Giften
und Strömen von Duft –

untergegangen im Meer
und aufgegangen im Himmel
die Erde!

VIII

…the earth, sea and sky.
Rooted up by kisses
the earth,
the sea and the sky.
Embraced by my words,
the earth,
still embraced by my last word,
the sea and the sky!

Plagued by my sounds
this earth,
that, sobbing in my teeth,
put down anchor
with all its furnaces, towers
and proud peaks,

this battered earth,
which before me uncovers its ravines,
its steppes, deserts and tundra,

this unresting earth,
with its quivering magnetic fields,
which bind it here
with unknown chains of power,

this stunned and stunning earth
grown thick with belladonna,
leaden poisons
and streams of perfume —

sunk in the sea
and risen in the sky
the earth!

IX

Die schwarze Katze,
das Öl auf dem Boden,
der böse Blick:

Unglück!

Zieh das Korallenhorn,
häng die Hörner vors Haus,
Dunkel, kein Licht!

X

O Liebe, die unsre Schalen
aufbrach und fortwarf, unseren Schild,
den Wetterschutz und braunen Rost von Jahren!

O Leiden, die unsre Liebe austraten,
ihr feuchtes Feuer in den fühlenden Teilen!
Verqualmt, verendend im Qualm, geht die Flamme in sich.

XI

Du willst das Wetterleuchten, wirfst die Messer,
du trennst der Luft die warmen Adern auf;

dich blendend, springen aus den offnen Pulsen
lautlos die letzten Feuerwerke auf:

Wahnsinn, Verachtung, dann die Rache,
und schon die Reue und der Widerruf.

IX

Black cat,
oil from the ground,
the evil glance:

Disaster!

Pull out the coral horn,
hang the horns before the house!
Darkness! No light!

X

O love, which broke open
and flung away our shells, our shield,
our shelters and the brown rust of years.

O sorrows, which stamped out our love,
its damp fire felt in tender places!
Filled with smoke, dying in smoke, the flame consumes itself.

XI

Wanting summer lightning, you throw the knife,
slicing through the air to the warmth of its veins;

blinding, as they spring up from open wounds,
are the soundless last fireworks you see displayed:

madness, contempt, and then revenge,
as remorse follows soon, and a cry of pain.

Du nimmst noch wahr, daß deine Klingen stumpfen,
und endlich fühlst du, wie die Liebe schließt:

mit ehrlichen Gewittern, reinem Atem.
Und sie verstößt dich in das Traumverlies.

Wo ihre goldnen Haare niederhängen,
greifst du nach ihr, der Leiter in das Nichts.

Tausend und eine Nacht hoch sind die Sprossen.
Der Schritt ins Leere ist der letzte Schritt.

Und wo du aufprallst, sind die alten Orte,
und jedem Ort gibst du drei Tropfen Blut.

Umnachtet hältst du wurzellose Locken.
Die Schelle läutet, und es ist genug.

XII

Mund, der in meinem Mund genächtigt hat,
Aug, das mein Aug bewachte,
Hand –

und die mich schleiften, die Augen!
Mund, der das Urteil sprach,
Hand, die mich hinrichtete!

You realize it's true, your sword is blunted,
and finally you feel just how love ends:

with raging storms, with purest breath,
and with you locked up inside the dream dungeon.

It's then that where love's golden hair hangs down,
the ladder to emptiness is what you'll be grasping,

for a thousand and one nights high are the rungs,
while the very last step is the step into nothing.

And there where you crash exist the old places,
and to each place you give three drops of blood.

Deranged, you only cling to rootless curls.
You hear the bell ring out, and it's enough.

XII

Mouth, which slept in my mouth,
Eye that guarded my own,
Hand –

and those eyes that drilled through me!
Mouth, which spoke the sentence,
Hand, which executed me!

XIII

Die Sonne wärmt nicht, stimmlos ist das Meer.
Die Gräber, schneeverpackt, schnürt niemand auf.
Wird denn kein Kohlenbecken angefüllt
mit fester Glut? Doch Glut tut's nicht.

Erlöse mich! Ich kann nicht länger sterben.

Der Heilige hat anderes zu tun;
er sorgt sich um die Stadt und geht ums Brot.
Die Wäscheleine trägt so schwer am Tuch;
bald wird es fallen. Doch mich deckt's nicht zu.

Ich bin noch schuldig. Heb mich auf.
Ich bin nicht schuldig. Heb mich auf.

Das Eiskorn lös vom zugefrornen Aug,
brich mit den Blicken ein,
die blauen Gründe such,
schwimm, schau und tauch:

Ich bin es nicht.
Ich bin's.

XIII

The sun gives no warmth, voiceless is the sea.
No one opens the graves packed in snow.
Is it because no brazier is filled
with glowing coals? Yet the glow does nothing.

Release me! I can no longer die.

The saint is busy elsewhere,
he is concerned with a city and bread.
The washline is heavy with linen;
soon it will fall. But it won't cover me.

I am still guilty. Raise me up.
I am not guilty. Raise me up.

Loosen the sliver of ice from the frozen eye,
break through with a piercing stare,
seek the blue depths,
swim, look and dive:

I am not the one.
I am.

XIV

Wart meinen Tod ab und dann hör mich wieder,
es kippt der Schneekorb, und das Wasser singt,
in die Toledo münden alle Töne, es taut,
ein Wohlklang schmilzt das Eis.
O großes Tauen!

Erwart dir viel!

Silben im Oleander,
Wort im Akaziengrün
Kaskaden aus der Wand.

Die Becken füllt,
hell und bewegt,
Musik.

XV

Die Liebe hat einen Triumph und der Tod hat einen,
die Zeit und die Zeit danach.
Wir haben keinen.

Nur Sinken um uns von Gestirnen. Abglanz und Schweigen.
Doch das Lied überm Staub danach
wird uns übersteigen.

XIV

Wait for my death, then hear me again.
Snowflakes will tumble and the water sing,
all sounds flow into the Toledo, its surface thawing,
a melody melting the ice.
Oh great thaw!

So much awaits you.

Syllables in oleander,
words in acacia green,
cascades from the wall.

The basins fill,
turbulent and clear,
with music.

XV

Love has its triumph and death has one,
in time and the time beyond us.
We have none.

Only the sinking of stars. Silence and reflection.
Yet the song beyond the dust
will overcome our own.

Gedichte 1948–1953

I Poems 1948 - 1953

[Abends frag ich meine Mutter]

Abends frag ich meine Mutter
heimlich nach dem Glockenläuten,
wie ich mir die Tage deuten
und die Nacht bereiten soll.

Tief im Grund verlang ich immer
alles restlos zu erzählen,
in Akkorden auszuwählen,
was an Klängen mich umspielt.

Leise lauschen wir zusammen:
meine Mutter träumt mich wieder,
und sie trifft, wie alte Lieder,
meines Wesens Dur und Moll.

[On Many Nights I Ask My Mother]

On many nights I ask my mother
furtively after the hours chime,
how I should learn to tell the time
and ready myself for the night.

In my inner depths, I always demand
that all be made completely clear,
picking out from the chords I hear
what confuses me within their strains.

Quietly we sit and listen together:
my mother dreams of what I'll be,
arranging, like any old melody,
my essential notes, major and minor.

[Wir gehen, die Herzen im Staub]

Wir gehen, die Herzen im Staub,
und lange schon hart am Versagen.
Man hört uns nur nicht, ist zu taub,
um das Stöhnen im Staub zu beklagen.

Wir singen, den Ton in der Brust.
Dort ist er noch niemals entsprungen.
Nur manchmal hat einer gewußt:
wir sind nicht zum Bleiben gezwungen.

Wir halten. Beenden den Trott.
Sonst ist auch das Ende verdorben.
Und richten die Augen auf Gott:
wir haben den Abschied erworben!

[We Leave, Hearts Sunk in Dust]

We leave, hearts sunk in dust,
long on the verge of failure.
Others are too deaf to hear us,
to call groans in dust out of order.

We sing, the sound in our breast.
From there it was never released.
Only sometimes did one attest
that remaining was never decreed.

We stop. We cease to trot.
Lest the end becomes a farce.
Our eyes are turned towards God:
we have been granted discharge.

[Es könnte viel bedeuten]

Es könnte viel bedeuten: wir vergehen,
wir kommen ungefragt und müssen weichen.
Doch daß wir sprechen und uns nicht verstehen
und keinen Augenblick des andern Hand erreichen,

zerschlägt so viel: wir werden nicht bestehen.
Schon den Versuch bedrohen fremde Zeichen,
und das Verlangen, tief uns anzusehen,
durchtrennt ein Kreuz, uns einsam auszustreichen.

[It Could Mean So Much]

It could mean so much: we cease to exist,
that we arrive unasked and then must yield.
That we speak, and yet misunderstanding persists,
and not for a moment is another's hand held   .

destroys so much: we will not survive.
Even strange signs forbid what we hold devout,
and the need for introspection that's still alive
a cross severs, as alone we're canceled out.

Entfremdung

In den Bäumen kann ich keine Bäume mehr sehen.
Die Äste haben nicht die Blätter, die sie in den Wind halten.
Die Früchte sind süß, aber ohne Liebe.
Sie sättigen nicht einmal.
Was soll nur werden?
Vor meinen Augen flieht der Wald,
vor meinem Ohr schließen die Vögel den Mund,
für mich wird keine Wiese zum Bett.
Ich bin satt vor der Zeit
und hungre nach ihr.
Was soll nur werden?

Auf den Bergen werden nachts die Feuer brennen.
Soll ich mich aufmachen, mich allem wieder nähern?

Ich kann in keinem Weg mehr einen Weg sehen.

Estrangement

Within the trees I no longer can see any trees.
The branches are bare of leaves, carried off by the wind.
The fruits are sweet, but empty of love.
They do not even satisfy.
What shall happen?
Before my eyes the forest flees,
bird song no longer reaching my ears,
and for me no pasture will become a bed.
I am full with time
yet hunger for it.
What shall happen?

Nightly upon the mountains the fires will burn.
Shall I prepare myself to draw near to them all again?

I can no longer see on any path a path.

Betrunkner Abend

Betrunkner Abend, voll vom blauen Licht,
taumelt ans Fenster und begehrt zu singen.
Die Scheiben drängen furchtsam sich und dicht,
in denen seine Schatten sich verfingen.

Er schwankt verdunkelnd um das Häusermeer,
trifft auf ein Kind, es schreiend zu verjagen,
und atmet keuchend hinter allem her,
Beängstigendes flüsternd auszusagen.

Im feuchten Hof am dunklen Mauerrand
tummelt mit Ratten er sich in den Ecken.
Ein Weib, in grau verschlissenem Gewand,
weicht vor ihm weg, sich tiefer zu verstecken.

Am Brunnen rinnt ein dünner Faden noch,
ein Tropfen läuft, den andern zu erhaschen;
dort trinkt er jäh aus rostverschleimtem Loch
und hilft, die schwarzen Gossen mitzuwaschen.

Betrunkner Abend, voll vom blauen Licht,
taumelt ins Fenster und beginnt zu singen.
Die Scheiben brechen. Blutend im Gesicht
dringt er herein, mit meinem Graun zu ringen.

Drunken Evening

The drunken evening, saturated with blue light,
staggers to the window to sing a ballad.
The panes press hard and thick against the sight,
as in the glass its shadows become entangled.

It slinks so darkly around the sea of houses,
grabs for a child, and shrieks to scare him away;
while after everyone, evening gasps for breath,
sounding a whispered alarm that gives it away.

In a damp farmyard, nearby the dark outer wall,
it scampers with the rats deep in the corners.
The woman wearing a ragged gray shawl,
skitters away to hide herself still deeper.

There's still a stream trickling from the well,
a drop that runs, trying to catch the first;
it has a quick drink there from a rusty pail,
and more from black gutters to ease its thirst.

The drunken evening, saturated with blue light,
staggers against the window and begins to sing.
Windowpanes shatter. Its bloodied face fights
its way inside, wrestling me down, still shuddering.

Hinter der Wand

Ich hänge als Schnee von den Zweigen
in den Frühling des Tals,
als kalte Quelle treibe ich im Wind,
feucht fall ich in die Blüten
als ein Tropfen,
um den sie faulen
wie um einen Sumpf.
Ich bin das Immerzu-ans-Sterben-Denken.

Ich fliege, denn ich kann nicht ruhig gehen,
durch aller Himmel sichere Gebäude
und stürze Pfeiler um und höhle Mauern.
Ich warne, denn ich kann des Nachts nicht schlafen,
die andern mit des Meeres fernem Rauschen.
Ich steige in den Mund der Wasserfälle,
und von den Bergen lös ich polterndes Geröll.

Ich bin der großen Weltangst Kind,
die in den Frieden und die Freude hängt
wie Glockenschläge in des Tages Schreiten
und wie die Sense in den reifen Acker.

Ich bin das Immerzu-ans-Sterben-Denken.

Behind the Wall

I hang as snow from the branches
in the valley of spring,
as a cold spell I float on the wind,
falling damp upon the blossoms
as a drop
in which they decay
as if sunk in a swamp.
I am the Continual-Thought-of-Dying.

Because I cannot walk firmly, I fly
through every sky above secure buildings
and knock down pillars and undermine walls.
Since I cannot sleep at night, I warn
others with the distant roar of the sea.
I pass through the mouth of waterfalls
and let topple from mountains the rumbling boulders.

I am the child of great fear for the world,
who within peace and joy hangs suspended
like the stroke of a bell in the day's passing
and like the scythe in the ripe pasture.

I am the Continual-Thought-Of-Dying.

[Beim Hufschlag der Nacht]

Beim Hufschlag der Nacht, des schwarzen Hengstes vorm
   Tor,
zittert mein Herz noch wie einst und reicht mir den Sattel
   im Flug,
rot wie das Halfter, das Diomedes mir lieh.
Gewaltig sprengt der Wind mir auf dunkler Straße voran
und teilt das schwarze Gelock der schlafenden Bäume,
daß die vom Mondlicht nassen Früchte
erschrocken auf Schulter und Schwert springen,
und ich schleudre
die Peitsche auf einen erloschenen Stern.
Nur einmal verhalt ich den Schritt, deine treulosen
   Lippen zu
küssen, schon fängt sich dein Haar in den Zügeln,
und dein Schuh schleift im Staub.

Und ich hör deinen Atem noch
und das Wort, mit dem du mich schlugst.

[At the Hoofbeat of Night]

At the hoofbeat of night, of the black stallion before
   the gate,
my heart flutters as it once did and offers me its saddle
   in flight,
red as the halter that Diomedes lent to me.
Powerfully the wind blows before me on the dark streets
and parts the black curls of the sleeping trees,
such that the fruits dripping with moonlight
fall and stun my shoulders and sword,
and I hurl
the whip towards an extinguished star.
Only once do I slow my stride, in order to kiss
   your unfaithful lips,
your hair becoming caught in the reins,
and your shoe dragging through the dust.

And I still hear your breathing
and the word with which you beat me.

Dem Abend gesagt

Meine Zweifel, bitter und ungestillt,
versickern in den Abendtiefen.
Müdigkeit singt an meinem Ohr.
Ich lausche . . .
Das war doch gestern schon!
Das kommt und geht doch wieder!

Die Schlafwege kenn ich bis ins süßeste Gefild.
Ich will dort nimmer gehen.
Noch weiß ich nicht, wo mir der dunkle See
die Qual vollendet.
Ein Spiegel soll dort liegen,
klar und dicht,
und will uns,
funkelnd vor Schmerz,
die Gründe zeigen.

Spoken to the Evening

My doubts, bitter and unappeased,
drain away in the evening's depths.
Weariness hums inside my ear.
I listen…
That's the way it was yesterday!
It comes and it goes again!

I know the paths to sleep lead to the sweetest field.
I never want to go there.
Yet I don't know where, for me, the dark lake
of torment will end.
A mirror shall lie there,
thick and clear,
and will show us,
sparkling with pain,
the deepest reasons.

Vision

Jetzt schon zum dritten Mal der Donnerschlag!
Und aus dem Meer taucht langsam Schiff auf Schiff.
Versunkne Schiffe mit verkohltem Mast,
versunkne Schiffe mit zerschossner Brust,
mit halbzerfetztem Leib.

Und schwimmen stumm,
unhörbar durch die Nacht.
Und keine Welle schließt sich hinter ihnen.

Sie haben keinen Weg, sie werden keinen finden,
kein Wind wird wagen, fest in sie zu greifen,
kein Hafen wird sich öffnen.
Der Leuchtturm kann sich schlafend stellen!

Wenn diese Schiffe bis ans Ufer kommen . . .
Nein, nicht ans Ufer!
Wir werden sterben wie die Fischzüge,
die rund um sie auf breiten Wogen wiegen
zu abertausend Leichen!

Vision

Now for the third time the clap of thunder!
And from the sea there surfaces vessel after vessel.
Sunken vessels, each with a charred mast,
sunken vessels, each with a breast shot through,
with a body half mangled.

And mutely they swim,
inaudible through the night.
And no wave drags them under.

They have no course, they will not find one,
no wind will venture to strongly grip them,
no harbor will open itself.
Even the lighthouse can stand there sleeping!

Until these vessels reach the shore…
No, not the shore!
We will die like the netted fish
that may twirl when swaying above the wide waves,
but are still a thousand corpses!

Menschenlos

Verwunschnes Wolkenschloß, in dem wir treiben . . .
Wer weiß, ob wir nicht schon durch viele Himmel
so ziehen mit verglasten Augen?
Wir, in die Zeit verbannt
und aus dem Raum gestoßen,
wir, Flieger durch die Nacht und Bodenlose.

Wer weiß, ob wir nicht schon um Gott geflogen,
weil wir pfeilschnell schäumten, ohne ihn zu sehen
und unsre Samen weiterschleuderten,
um in noch dunkleren Geschlechtern fortzuleben,
jetzt schuldhaft treiben?

Wer weiß, ob wir nicht lange, lang schon sterben?
Der Wolkenball mit uns strebt immer höher.
Die dünne Luft lähmt heute schon die Hände.
Und wenn die Stimme bricht und unser Atem steht?

Bleibt die Verwunschenheit für letzte Augenblicke?

Destiny

Enchanted cloud castle in which we're suspended...
Who knows if we have not already moved
through many heavens with glazed eyes?
We, who are banished from time
and thrust from space,
we, who are refugees in the night and exiled.

Who knows if we have not flown past God,
for we fly off, swift as an arrow, without seeing Him
and only cast our seeds wider
in order to live on through darker lineage,
suspended and guilty.

Who knows if we died recently or long ago?
The fireball containing us strains ever higher.
The thin air today makes the hands lame.
And what if our voice should snap and our breathing stop?

Does enchantment remain for final instants?

Wie soll ich mich nennen?

Einmal war ich ein Baum und gebunden,
dann entschlüpft ich als Vogel und war frei,
in einen Graben gefesselt gefunden,
entließ mich berstend ein schmutziges Ei.

Wie halt ich mich? Ich habe vergessen,
woher ich komme und wohin ich geh,
ich bin von vielen Leibern besessen,
ein harter Dorn und ein flüchtendes Reh.

Freund bin ich heute den Ahornzweigen,
morgen vergehe ich mich an dem Stamm . . .
Wann begann die Schuld ihren Reigen,
mit dem ich von Samen zu Samen schwamm?

Aber in mir singt noch ein Beginnen
– oder ein Enden – und wehrt meiner Flucht,
ich will dem Pfeil dieser Schuld entrinnen,
der mich in Sandkorn und Wildente sucht.

Vielleicht kann ich mich einmal erkennen,
eine Taube einen rollenden Stein . . .
Ein Wort nur fehlt! Wie soll ich mich nennen,
ohne in anderer Sprache zu sein.

How Shall I Name Myself?

Once I was a tree that had been bound,
and then I slipped out as a free bird;
chained up in a ditch I was later found,
laying an egg that was covered with dirt.

What am I now? I have forgotten
from where I come and where I'm headed,
in several bodies I live on,
a hard thorn and the deer that fled.

Today I befriend the maple branch,
tomorrow I will wound its trunk…
When did guilt begin its own round dance
by which I drifted from trunk to trunk.

But a beginning sings inside me still
– or an end – and it prevents my escape,
I will evade this arrow of guilt
that in sand grains, wild ducks, seeks my shape.

Perhaps I can once more see myself,
maybe a dove a rolling stone…
Words fail! How shall I name myself
without living in another tongue.

[Die Häfen waren geöffnet]

Die Häfen waren geöffnet. Wir schifften uns ein,
die Segel voraus, den Traum über Bord,
Stahl an den Knien und Lachen um unsere Haare,
denn unsere Ruder trafen ins Meer, schneller als Gott.

Unsere Ruder schlugen die Schaufeln Gottes und teilten
    die Flut;
vorne war Tag, und hinten blieben die Nächte,
oben war unser Stern, und unten versanken die andern,
draußen verstummte der Sturm, und drinnen wuchs unsre
    Faust.

Erst als ein Regen entbrannte, lauschten wir wieder;
Speere stürzten herab und Engel traten hervor,
hefteten schwärzere Augen in unsere schwarzen.
Vernichtet standen wir da. Unser Wappen flog auf:

Ein Kreuz im Blut und ein größeres Schiff überm Herzen.

[The Harbors Were Open]

The harbors were open. We boarded the ships,
the sails were unfurled, the dream tossed overboard,
a sword across the knees and laughter in our hair,
because our oars dipped into the sea faster than God.

Our oars beat like the oars of God and parted the flood;
ahead was day, and behind remained the nights,
above us was our star, and below the others sank away,
while outside the storm ceased, and inside our fists
  were clenched.

Only when a rainstorm burst did we listen again;
spears fell all around and angels appeared,
blacker eyes fixed upon our own black eyes.
We stood there devastated. Our heraldry soaring:

A cross of blood and a larger ship above our hearts.

[Die Welt ist weit]

Die Welt ist weit und die Wege von Land zu Land,
und der Orte sind viele, ich habe alle gekannt,
ich habe von allen Türmen Städte gesehen,
die Menschen, die kommen werden und die schon gehen.
Weit waren die Felder von Sonne und Schnee,
zwischen Schienen und Straßen, zwischen Berg und See.
Und der Mund der Welt war weit und voll Stimmen an
    meinem Ohr
und schrieb, noch des Nachts, die Gesänge der Vielfalt vor.
Den Wein aus fünf Bechern trank ich in einem Zuge aus,
mein nasses Haar trocknen vier Winde in ihrem
    wechselnden Haus.

Die Fahrt ist zu Ende,
doch ich bin mit nichts zu Ende gekommen,
jeder Ort hat ein Stück von meinem Lieben genommen,
jedes Licht hat mir ein Aug verbrannt,
in jedem Schatten zerriß mein Gewand.

Die Fahrt ist zu Ende.
Noch bin ich mit jeder Ferne verkettet,
doch kein Vogel hat mich über die Grenzen gerettet,
kein Wasser, das in die Mündung zieht,
treibt mein Gesicht, das nach unten sieht,
treibt meinen Schlaf, der nicht wandern will . . .
Ich weiß die Welt näher und still.

[The World is Far and Wide]

The world is far and wide, and the roads from land to land,
there are many in each place, which I've seen firsthand;
from inside every tower, I have seen the cities,
the people who are coming, the people who've left already.
The fields were so immense with sun and snow,
between the mountain and lake, the tracks and roads.
And the mouth of the world was wide, full of voices
  at my ear that transcribed,
not only at night, the songs of the diversified.
I drank down five cups of wine in a single sitting,
the four winds dried my hair in their house that is
  ever-changing.

Now the journey is over,
and yet with nothing I've come to the end,
a piece of my beloved each place has taken,
my eyes have been scorched by each light they've borne,
in every shadow my dress has been torn.

Now the journey is over.
Yet to every distance I'm still bound,
though no bird has lifted me over the border beyond,
no water, drifting towards the sea's mouth,
carries my face, that still looks down,
nor my sleep, which does not want to travel…
I know the world that's nearer and still.

Hinter der Welt wird ein Baum stehen
mit Blättern aus Wolken
und einer Krone aus Blau.
In seine Rinde aus rotem Sonnenband
schneidet der Wind unser Herz
und kühlt es mit Tau.

Hinter der Welt wird ein Baum stehen,
eine Frucht in den Wipfeln,
mit einer Schale aus Gold.
Laß uns hinübersehen,
wenn sie im Herbst der Zeit
in Gottes Hände rollt!

Behind the world a tree shall stand
with leaves that are clouds
and a crown that is blue.
With a red sunbeam the wind now carves
our heart into its bark
and cools it with dew.

Behind the world a tree shall stand,
a fruit at its top
with skin of gold.
Let us see beyond,
in the autumn of time,
when into God's hands it rolls.

[Noch fürcht ich]

Noch fürcht ich, dich mit dem Garn meines Atems zu
   binden,
dich zu gewanden mit den blauen Fahnen des Traums,
an den Nebeltoren meines finsteren Schlosses
Fackeln zu brennen, daß du mich fändest . . .

Noch fürcht ich, dich aus schimmernden Tagen zu lösen,
aus dem goldnen Gefälle des Sonnenflusses der Zeit,
wenn über dem schrecklichen Antlitz des Monds
silbrig mein Herz schäumt.

Blick auf und sieh mich nicht an!
Es sinken die Fahnen, verflammt sind die Fackeln,
und der Mond beschreibt seine Bahn.
Es ist Zeit, daß du kommst und mich hältst, heiliger Wahn!

[I'm Still Afraid]

I'm still afraid to snare you with my breath,
drape you with blue banners of the dream,
or outside the misty door of my darkened castle,
burn torches, such that you'd find me…

I'm still afraid to free you from shimmering days,
from the river bed of time's own river of sun,
fearing my heart would burst silvery above the moon's
own frightening countenance.

Look up and don't look at me!
The banners are sinking, the torches have been lit,
the moon follows the course it traces.
It's time you came to seize me, holy madness!

Beweis zu nichts

Weißt du, Mutter, wenn die Breiten und Längen
den Ort nicht nennen, daß deine Kinder
aus dem dunklen Winkel der Welt dir winken?
Du bleibst stehn, wo sich die Wege verschlingen,
und vorrätig ist dein Herz vor jedem andern.
Wir reichen nicht lange, werfen mit Werken um uns
und blicken zurück. Doch der Rauch überm Herd
läßt uns das Feuer nicht sehn.

Frag: kommt keines wieder? Vom Lot abwärts geführt,
nicht in Richtung des Himmels, fördern wir
Dinge zutage, in denen Vernichtung wohnt und Kraft,
uns zu zerstreuen. Dies alles ist ein Beweis
zu nichts und von niemand verlangt. Entfachst du
das Feuer von neuem, erscheinen wir unkenntlich,
geschwärzte Gesichter, deinem weißen Gesicht.
Wein! Aber winke uns nicht.

Proof of Nothing

Do you know, mother, when latitude and longitude
can't locate a village, your children wave
to you from the dark corners of the world?
You stand there, where the paths twist around you,
and your heart is reserved for everyone else.
We don't stay for long, heading off to work
and glancing back. Yet the mist above the hearth
prevents us seeing the fire.

Ask yourself: will anyone return? Having left the straight
and narrow path, and not for heaven, we bring to light
things in which there lives destruction and the power
to scatter us to the wind. All this is proof
of nothing and none demands it. For when you kindle
the fire anew, we will appear unrecognizable,
before your own pale face, our faces black.
Weep! But don't wave back.

Gedichte 1957–1961

II Poems 1957 - 1961

Bruderschaft

Alles ist Wundenschlagen,
und keiner hat keinem verziehn.
Verletzt wie du und verletzend,
lebte ich auf dich hin.

Die reine, die Geistberührung,
um jede Berührung vermehrt,
wir erfahren sie alternd,
ins kälteste Schweigen gekehrt.

Brotherhood

Everyone carries a wound,
and none has forgiven another.
Wounded as you, and wounding,
it was you that I lived for.

The pure touch of the spirit,
increasing the weight of each touch,
we come to know when aging,
by the coldest silence clutched.

[Verordnet diesem Geschlecht keinen Glauben]

Verordnet diesem Geschlecht keinen Glauben,
genug sind Sterne, Schiffe und Rauch,
es legt sich in die Dinge, bestimmt
Sterne und die unendliche Zahl,
und ein Zug tritt, nenn ihn Zug einer Liebe,
reiner aus allem hervor.

Die Himmel hängen welk und Sterne lösen
sich aus der Verknüpfung mit Mond und Nacht.

[Prescribe No Belief]

Prescribe no belief for this generation,
stars are enough, ships and smoke;
they appropriate all things, certifying
stars and their endless number,
and a procession begins, let's say the procession
of love, all the more purely.

The heavens hang limp and the stars release
themselves from their bond with the moon and night.

Hôtel de la Paix

Die Rosenlast stürzt lautlos von den Wänden,
und durch den Teppich scheinen Grund und Boden.
Das Lichtherz bricht der Lampe.
Dunkel. Schritte.
Der Riegel hat sich vor den Tod geschoben.

Hôtel de la Paix

The weight of roses falls silently from the walls,
and through the carpet shine the floor and earth.
The light's heart breaks within the lamp.
Darkness. Steps.
The bolt is thrown as death comes knocking.

Exil

Ein Toter bin ich der wandelt
gemeldet nirgends mehr
unbekannt im Reich des Präfekten
überzählig in den goldenen Städten
und im grünenden Land

abgetan lange schon
und mit nichts bedacht

Nur mit Wind mit Zeit und mit Klang

der ich unter Menschen nicht leben kann

Ich mit der deutschen Sprache
dieser Wolke um mich
die ich halte als Haus
treibe durch alle Sprachen

O wie sie sich verfinstert
die dunklen die Regentöne
nur die wenigen fallen

In hellere Zonen trägt dann sie den Toten hinauf

Exile

I am a dead man who wanders
registered nowhere
unknown in the prefect's realm
unaccounted for in the golden cities
and the greening land

long since given up
and provided with nothing

Only with wind with time and with sound

I who cannot live among humans

I with the German language
this cloud around me
which I keep as a house
press through all languages

Oh how it grows dark
those muted those rain tones
only a few fall

Into brighter zones it will lift the dead man up

Nach dieser Sintflut

Nach dieser Sintflut
möchte ich die Taube,
und nichts als die Taube,
noch einmal gerettet sehn.

Ich ginge ja unter in diesem Meer!
flög' sie nicht aus,
brächte sie nicht
in letzter Stunde das Blatt.

After This Flood

After this flood
I'd like to see the dove,
and nothing but the dove,
be rescued once more.

I'd drown in this sea!
if she didn't fly out,
if she didn't bring,
in the last hour, the leaf.

Mirjam

Woher hast du dein dunkles Haar genommen,
den süßen Namen mit dem Mandelton?
Nicht weil du jung bist, glänzt du so von Morgen –
dein Land ist Morgen, tausend Jahre schon.

Versprich uns Jericho, weck auf den Psalter,
die Jordanquelle gib aus deiner Hand
und laß die Mörder überrascht versteinen
und einen Augenblick dein zweites Land!

An jede Steinbrust rühr und tu das Wunder,
daß auch den Stein die Träne überrinnt.
Und laß dich taufen mit dem heißen Wasser.
Bleib uns nur fremd, bis wir uns fremder sind.

Oft wird ein Schnee in deine Wiege fallen.
Unter den Kufen wird ein Eiston sein.
Doch wenn du tief schläfst, ist die Welt bezwungen.
Das rote Meer zieht seine Wasser ein!

Mirjam

From where did you get your hair that is so raven,
as well as that sweet name that sounds like almonds?
It's not mere youth that makes you look like morning –
your land is made young, and will be for a millennium.

Promise us Jericho, awaken the psalter's tones,
let the waters of Jordan flow from your hand;
have the murderers ambushed and turned to stone,
and, for a moment, have your second land.

Touch hearts of stone, perform a miracle's wonder,
such that even the stone by tears is overrun.
Let yourself be baptized by the scalding water.
Remain an enigma, until we are joined as one.

Snow will often fall into your cradle.
There will be the sound of ice beneath the runners.
Yet when you soundly sleep the world is quelled.
The red sea will then part its very waters!

Strömung

So weit im Leben und so nah am Tod,
daß ich mit niemand darum rechten kann,
reiß ich mir von der Erde meinen Teil;

dem stillen Ozean stoß ich den grünen Keil
mitten ins Herz und schwemm mich selber an.

Zinnvögel steigen auf und Zimtgeruch!
Mit meinem Mörder Zeit bin ich allein.
In Rausch und Bläue puppen wir uns ein.

Stream

So far in life and yet so near to death
that there's no one I can argue with now,
I rip from the earth my separate part;

I thrust its green wedge into the heart
of the calm ocean, as I wash aground.

Tin birds rise and cinnamon scents!
With my murderer, Time, I'm alone.
Drunk and blue we spin our cocoon.

Geh, Gedanke

Geh, Gedanke, solang ein zum Flug klares Wort
dein Flügel ist, dich aufhebt und dorthin geht,
wo die leichten Metalle sich wiegen,
wo die Luft schneidend ist
in einem neuen Verstand,
wo Waffen sprechen
von einziger Art.
Verficht uns dort!

Die Woge trug ein Treibholz hoch und sinkt.
Das Fieber riß dich an sich, läßt dich fallen.
Der Glaube hat nur einen Berg versetzt.

Laß stehn, was steht, geh, Gedanke!,

von nichts andrem als unsrem Schmerz durchdrungen.
Entsprich uns ganz!

Leave, Thought

Leave, thought, for as long as a word cleared for flight
is your wing, it lifts you and goes
where the light metals sway,
where the air is piercing
within a new understanding,
where weapons speak
of a single means.
Defend us there!

The wave bore driftwood high and now sinks.
Fever took hold of you, now it lets you fall.
Faith has moved no more than a mountain.

Let stand what stands, leave, thought!,

penetrated by nothing other than our pain.
Stand for all we are!

Liebe: Dunkler Erdteil

Der schwarze König zeigt die Raubtiernägel,
zehn blasse Monde jagt er in die Bahn,
und er befiehlt den großen Tropenregen.
Die Welt sieht dich vom andren Ende an!

Es zieht dich übers Meer an jene Küsten
aus Gold und Elfenbein, an seinen Mund.
Dort aber liegst du immer auf den Knien,
und er verwirft und wählt dich ohne Grund.

Und er befiehlt die große Mittagswende.
Die Luft zerbricht, das grün und blaue Glas,
die Sonne kocht den Fisch im seichten Wasser,
und um die Büffelherde brennt das Gras.

Ins Jenseits ziehn geblendet Karawanen,
und er peitscht Dünen durch das Wüstenland,
er will dich sehn mit Feuer an den Füßen.
Aus deinen Striemen fließt der rote Sand.

Er, fellig, farbig, ist an deiner Seite,
er greift dich auf, wirft über dich sein Garn.
Um deine Hüften knüpfen sich Lianen,
um deinen Hals kraust sich der fette Farn.

Aus allen Dschungelnischen: Seufzer, Schreie.
Er hebt den Fetisch. Dir entfällt das Wort.
Die süßen Hölzer rühren dunkle Trommeln.
Du blickst gebannt auf deinen Todesort.

Love: The Dark Continent

The black king holds aloft the panther's claws
and chases ten pale moons around like prey,
invoking great tropical rain that begins to fall.
The world is looking at you in a different way!

You're drawn across the sea and to those coasts
of gold and ivory, and onward towards his mouth.
But there you always fall upon your knees,
for he chooses and rejects you without grounds.

Yet he's the one who orders the day to change.
The air shatters, pieces of green and blue glass,
as the hot sun boils the fish in shallow water,
and around the buffalo herd it burns the grass.

Into another world, the shimmering caravans move,
he lashes at the dunes across the desert land,
for he wants to see fire burning at your feet,
as from your welts there flows the bright red sand.

He, hairy, brightly colored, is by your side;
he snatches you up, throws over you his snare.
Soon long liana ropes will bind your hips,
your throat is ruffled with a lush fern collar.

From every jungle recess: sighs and screams.
He lifts the fetish. You have no reply.
Sweet wooden sticks begin to beat dark drums.
You stare transfixed, seeing where you will die.

Sieh, die Gazellen schweben in den Lüften,
auf halbem Wege hält der Dattelschwarm!
Tabu ist alles: Erden, Früchte, Ströme . . .
Die Schlange hängt verchromt an deinem Arm.

Er gibt Insignien aus seinen Händen.
Trag die Korallen, geh im hellen Wahn!
Du kannst das Reich um seinen König bringen,
du, selbst geheim, blick sein Geheimnis an.

Um den Äquator sinken alle Schranken.
Der Panther steht allein im Liebesraum.
Er setzt herüber aus dem Tal des Todes,
und seine Pranke schleift den Himmelssaum.

Look, gazelles are floating on the breeze,
only halfway down bends the date's ripe swarm!
Everything is taboo: earth, fruit, streams…
The snake hangs shimmering upon your arm.

He gives to you insignia from his hands.
Wear the corals, walk in deluded raiment!
You can deprive the kingdom of its king,
for it's you who, secretly, has seen his secret.

On the equator all barriers are lowered.
The panther lives alone by love's own laws.
He crosses over from the valley of death,
trailing the heavens' fabric in his claws.

Aria I

Wohin wir uns wenden im Gewitter der Rosen,
ist die Nacht von Dornen erhellt, und der Donner
des Laubs, das so leise war in den Büschen,
folgt uns jetzt auf dem Fuß.

Wo immer gelöscht wird, was die Rosen entzünden,
schwemmt Regen uns in den Fluß. O fernere Nacht!
Doch ein Blatt, das uns traf, treibt auf den Wellen
bis zur Mündung uns nach.

Aria I

Wherever we turn in the storm of roses,
the night is lit up by thorns, and the thunder
of leaves, once so quiet within the bushes,
rumbling at our heels.

Wherever the fire of roses is extinguished,
rain washes us into the river. O distant night!
Yet a leaf, which once touched us, follows us on waves
towards the river's mouth.

Freies Geleit (Aria II)

Mit schlaftrunkenen Vögeln
und winddurchschossenen Bäumen
steht der Tag auf, und das Meer
leert einen schäumenden Becher auf ihn

Die Flüsse wallen ans große Wasser,
und das Land legt Liebesversprechen
der reinen Luft in den Mund
mit frischen Blumen.

Die Erde will keinen Rauchpilz tragen,
kein Geschöpf ausspeien vorm Himmel,
mit Regen und Zornesblitzen abschaffen
die unerhörten Stimmen des Verderbens.

Mit uns will sie die bunten Brüder
und grauen Schwestern erwachen sehn,
den König Fisch, die Hoheit Nachtigall
und den Feuerfürsten Salamander.

Für uns pflanzt sie Korallen ins Meer.
Wäldern befiehlt sie, Ruhe zu halten,
dem Marmor, die schöne Ader zu schwellen,
noch einmal dem Tau, über die Asche zu gehn.

Die Erde will ein freies Geleit ins All
jeden Tag aus der Nacht haben,
daß noch tausend und ein Morgen wird
von der alten Schönheit jungen Gnaden.

Safe Conduct (Aria II)

With birds drunk with sleep
and trees shot through with wind
the day awakens, and the sea empties
a foaming cup to honor it.

Rivers surge towards the wide water,
and the land lays loving vows
of pure air inside the mouth
with its fresh flowers.

The Earth will have no mushroom cloud,
no creature spits in the face of heaven,
with rain and thunderbolts it abolishes
the unbearable voice of destruction.

In us it wants the lively brothers
and to see the gray sisters awakened,
the King of Fish, the Royal Nightingale,
and, Prince of Fire, the Salamander.

For us it plants corals in the sea.
It orders forests to maintain the quiet,
for marble to swell its beautiful veins,
and once more for dew to settle on ashes.

Earth wants safe conduct in its orbit,
each day we have in the face of night,
so that ancient beauty as renewed graces
on a thousand and one mornings will rise.

Ihr Worte

Für Nelly Sachs, die Freundin, die Dichterin, in Verehrung

Ihr Worte, auf, mir nach!,
und sind wir auch schon weiter,
zu weit gegangen, geht's noch einmal
weiter, zu keinem Ende geht's.

Es hellt nicht auf.

Das Wort
wird doch nur
andre Worte nach sich ziehn,
Satz den Satz.
So möchte Welt,
endgültig,
sich aufdrängen,
schon gesagt sein.
Sagt sie nicht.

Worte, mir nach,
daß nicht endgültig wird
– nicht diese Wortbegier
und Spruch auf Widerspruch!

Laßt eine Weile jetzt.
keins der Gefühle sprechen,
den Muskel Herz
sich anders üben.

Laßt, sag ich, laßt.

You Words

for Nelly Sachs, friend and poet, in reverence

You words, arise, follow me!,
and though already we have gone farther,
gone too far, once more it goes
farther, to no end it goes.

It doesn't brighten.

The word
will only drag
other words behind it,
the sentence a sentence.
So the world wishes,
ultimately,
to press its own cause,
to already be spoken.
Do not speak it.

Words, follow me,
so nothing will be final
– not this passion for words,
nor a saying and its contradiction!

Let there be for now
no feeling expressed,
let the heart's muscle
exercise in another way.

Let be, I say, let be.

Ins höchste Ohr nicht,
nichts, sag ich, geflüstert,
zum Tod fall dir nichts ein,
laß, und mir nach, nicht mild
noch bitterlich,
nicht trostreich,
ohne Trost
bezeichnend nicht,
so auch nicht zeichenlos –

Und nur nicht dies: das Bild
im Staubgespinst, leeres Geroll
von Silben, Sterbenswörter.

Kein Sterbenswort,
Ihr Worte!

Into the highest ear
whisper, I say, nothing,
don't collapse into death,
let be, and follow me, not mild
nor bitter,
nor comforting,
without consolation
without significance,
and thus without symbols —

Most of all not this: the image
cobwebbed with dust, the empty rumble
of syllables, dying words.

Not a syllable,
you words!

Gedichte 1964–1967

III Poems 1964 - 1967

Wahrlich

Für Anna Achmatova

Wem es ein Wort nie verschlagen hat,
und ich sage es euch,
wer bloß sich zu helfen weiß
und mit den Worten –

dem ist nicht zu helfen.
Über den kurzen Weg nicht
und nicht über den langen.

Einen einzigen Satz haltbar zu machen,
auszuhalten in dem Bimbam von Worten.

Es schreibt diesen Satz keiner,
der nicht unterschreibt.

Truly

for Anna Akhmatova

To one who's never been stunned by a word,
and I say it to you all,
who only knows how to help himself
and only with words –

he cannot be helped.
Not over the short term
and not over the long.

To create a single lasting sentence,
to persevere in the ding-dong of words.

No one writes this sentence
who does not sign her name.

Böhmen liegt am Meer

Sind hierorts Häuser grün, tret ich noch in ein Haus.
Sind hier die Brücken heil, geh ich auf gutem Grund.
Ist Liebesmüh in alle Zeit verloren, verlier ich sie hier gern.

Bin ich's nicht, ist es einer, der ist so gut wie ich.

Grenzt hier ein Wort an mich, so laß ich's grenzen.
Liegt Böhmen noch am Meer, glaub ich den Meeren
    wieder.
Und glaub ich noch ans Meer, so hoffe ich auf Land.

Bin ich's, so ist's ein jeder, der ist soviel wie ich.
Ich will nichts mehr für mich. Ich will zugrunde gehn.

Zugrund – das heißt zum Meer, dort find ich Böhmen
    wieder.
Zugrund gerichtet, wach ich ruhig auf.
Von Grund auf weiß ich jetzt, und ich bin unverloren.

Kommt her, ihr Böhmen alle, Seefahrer, Hafenhuren und
    Schiffe
unverankert. Wollt ihr nicht böhmisch sein, Illyrer,
    Veroneser,
und Venezianer alle. Spielt die Komödien, die lachen
    machen

Und die zum Weinen sind. Und irrt euch hundertmal,
wie ich mich irrte und Proben nie bestand,
doch hab ich sie bestanden, ein um das andre Mal.

Bohemia Lies by the Sea

If houses here are green, I'll step inside a house.
If bridges here are sound, I'll walk on solid ground.
If love's labour's lost in every age, I'd gladly lose it here.

If it's not me, it's one who is as good as me.

If a word here borders on me, I'll let it border.
If Bohemia still lies by the sea, I'll believe in the sea again.
And believing in the sea, thus I can hope for land.

If it's me, then it's anyone, for he's as worthy as me.
I want nothing more for myself. I want to go under.

Under – that means the sea, there I'll find Bohemia again.
From my grave, I wake in peace.
From deep down I know now, and I'm not lost.

Come here, all you Bohemians, seafarers, dock whores, and ships
unanchored. Don't you want to be Bohemians, all you Illyrians,
Veronese and Venetians. Play the comedies that make us laugh

until we cry. And err a hundred times,
as I erred and never withstood the trials,
though I did withstand them time after time.

Wie Böhmen sie bestand und eines schönen Tags
ans Meer begnadigt wurde und jetzt am Wasser liegt.

Ich grenz noch an ein Wort und an ein andres Land,
ich grenz, wie wenig auch, an alles immer mehr,

ein Böhme, ein Vagant, der nichts hat, den nichts hält,
begabt nur noch, vom Meer, das strittig ist, Land meiner
    Wahl zu sehen.

As Bohemia withstood them and one fine day
was released to the sea and now lies by water.

I still border on a word and on another land,
I border, like little else, on everything more and more,

a Bohemian, a wandering minstrel, who has nothing, who
is held by nothing, gifted only at seeing, by a doubtful sea,
    the land of my choice.

Prag Jänner 64

Seit jener Nacht
gehe und spreche ich wieder,
böhmisch klingt es,
als wär ich wieder zuhause,

wo zwischen der Moldau, der Donau
und meinem Kindheitsfluß
alles einen Begriff von mir hat.

Gehen, schrittweis ist es wiedergekommen,
Sehen, angeblickt, habe ich wieder erlernt.

Gebückt noch, blinzelnd,
hing ich am Fenster,
sah die Schattenjahre,
in denen kein Stern
mir in den Mund hing,
sich über den Hügel entfernen.

Über den Hradschin
haben um sechs Uhr morgens
die Schneeschaufler aus der Tatra
mit ihren rissigen Pranken
die Scherben dieser Eisdecke gekehrt.

Unter den berstenden Blöcken
meines, auch meines Flusses
kam das befreite Wasser hervor.

Zu hören bis zum Ural.

Prague, January '64

Since that night
I walk and speak anew,
sounding Bohemian,
as if I were home again,

where between the Moldau, the Danube
and my childhood river,
I saw everything as my own.

Walking, it's all come back step by step;
seeing, observed, I've learned again.

Bent over, blinking,
I hung by the window,
saw the shadowy years
withdraw over the hill
in which no star
hung in my mouth.

Across the Hradčany,
at six in the morning,
Tatra snow shovelers
with their chapped paws
cleared away the icy shards.

Beneath the shattered slabs
of my, my river too,
the liberated water appeared.

Audible as far as the Urals.

Eine Art Verlust

Gemeinsam benutzt: Jahreszeiten, Bücher und eine Musik.
Die Schlüssel, die Teeschalen, den Brotkorb, Leintücher
    und ein Bett.
Eine Aussteuer von Worten, von Gesten, mitgebracht,
    verwendet, verbraucht.
Eine Hausordnung beachtet. Gesagt. Getan. Und immer
    die Hand gereicht.

In Winter, in ein Wiener Septett und in Sommer habe ich
    mich verliebt.
In Landkarten, in ein Bergnest, in einen Strand und in
    ein Bett.
Einen Kult getrieben mit Daten, Versprechen für
    unkündbar erklärt,
angehimmelt ein Etwas und fromm gewesen vor einem
    Nichts,

(– der gefalteten Zeitung, der kalten Asche, dem Zettel
    mit einer Notiz)
furchtlos in der Religion, denn die Kirche war dieses Bett.

Aus dem Seeblick hervor ging meine unerschöpfliche
    Malerei.
Von dem Balkon herab waren die Völker, meine Nachbarn,
    zu grüßen.
Am Kaminfeuer, in der Sicherheit, hatte mein Haar seine
    äußerste Farbe.
Das Klingeln an der Tür war der Alarm für meine Freude.

Nicht dich habe ich verloren,
sondern die Welt.

A Type of Loss

Commonly used: seasons, books and music.
The keys, the tea cups, the breadbasket, sheets
  and a bed.
A dowry of words, of gestures, brought along,
  used, spent.
Social manners observed. Said. Done. And always
  the hand extended.

With winter, a Vienna septet and with summer I've
  been in love.
With maps, a mountain hut, with a beach and
  a bed.
A cult filled with dates, promises
  impossibly given,
enthused about Something and pious before Nothing,

(– the folded newspapers, cold ashes, the slip of paper
  with a jotted note)
fearless in religion, as the church was this bed.

From the seascape came my inexhaustible painting.
From the balcony, the people, my neighbors,
  were there to be greeted.
By the fire, in safety, my hair had its most exceptional
  color.
The doorbell ringing was the alarm for my joy.

It was not you I lost,
but the world.

Enigma

Für Hans Werner Henze aus der Zeit der Ariosi

Nichts mehr wird kommen.

Frühling wird nicht mehr werden.
Tausendjährige Kalender sagen es jedem voraus.

Aber auch Sommer und weiterhin, was so gute Namen
wie »sommerlich« hat –
es wird nichts mehr kommen.

Du sollst ja nicht weinen,
sagt eine Musik.

Sonst
sagt
niemand
etwas.

Enigma

for Hans Werner Henze at the time of *Ariosi*

Nothing more will come.

Spring will no longer flourish.
Millennial calendars forecast it already.

But also summer and more, sweet words
such as "summer-like" –
nothing more will come.

You mustn't cry,
says the music.

Otherwise
no one
says
anything.

Keine Delikatessen

Nichts mehr gefällt mir.

Soll ich
eine Metapher ausstaffieren
mit einer Mandelblüte?
die Syntax kreuzigen
auf einen Lichteffekt?
Wer wird sich den Schädel zerbrechen
über so überflüssige Dinge –

Ich habe ein Einsehn gelernt
mit den Worten,
die da sind
(für die unterste Klasse)

Hunger
            Schande
                        Tränen
und
                        Finsternis.

Mit dem ungereinigten Schluchzen,
mit der Verzweiflung
(und ich verzweifle noch vor Verzweiflung)
über das viele Elend,
den Krankenstand, die Lebenskosten,
werde ich auskommen.

No Delicacies

Nothing pleases me anymore.

Should I
fit out a metaphor
with an almond blossom?
crucify the syntax
upon an effect of light?
Who will rack their brains
over such superfluous things –

I have learned an insight
with words
that exist
(for the lowest class)

Hunger
      Shame
            Tears
and
               Darkness.

With unpurged tears,
with despair
(and I despair in the face of despair)
about so much misery,
the many sick, the cost of living,
I will get by.

Ich vernachlässige nicht die Schrift,
sondern mich.
Die andern wissen sich
weißgott
mit den Worten zu helfen.
Ich bin nicht mein Assistent.

Soll ich
einen Gedanken gefangennehmen,
abführen in eine erleuchtete Satzzelle?
Aug und Ohr verköstigen
mit Worthappen erster Güte?
erforschen die Libido eines Vokals,
ermitteln die Liebhaberwerte unserer Konsonanten?

Muß ich
mit dem verhagelten Kopf,
mit dem Schreibkrampf in dieser Hand,
unter dreihundertnächtigem Druck
einreißen das Papier,
wegfegen die angezettelten Wortopern,
vernichtend so: ich du und er sie es

wir ihr?

(Soll doch. Sollen die andern.)

Mein Teil, es soll verloren gehen.

I don't neglect writing,
but rather myself.
The others are able
God knows
to get by with words.
I am not my assistant.

Should I
arrest an idea, lead it off
to a bright sentence cell?
feed sight and hearing
with first-class word morsels?
analyze the libido of a vowel,
estimate the collector's value of our consonants?

Must I
with a battered head,
with the writing cramp in this hand,
under the pressure of the three hundredth night
rip up the paper,
sweep away the scribbled word operas,
annihilating as well: I you and he she it

we you all?

(Should? The others should.)

My part, it shall be lost.

¹ See Bachmann's 1971 interview with Gerda Bödefeld in *Ingeborg Bachmann. Wir müssen wahre Sätze finden: Gespräche und Interviews*, eds. Christine Koschel and Inge von Weidenbaum, (Munich: Piper, 1983) 111-115.

² Hans E. Holthusen. "Kämpfender Sprachgeist. Die Lyrik Ingeborg Bachmanns," in *Kein objektives Urteil − nur ein lebendiges*, eds. Christine Koschel und Inge von Weidenbaum (Munich: Piper, 1989) 25 (my translation). Besides Holthusen's seminal essay, this volume collects together some of the most important criticism on Bachmann in German from the last forty years.

3 *Ingeborg Bachmann. Werke*, eds. Christine Koschel, Inge von Weidenbaum, and Clemens Münster, (Munich: Piper, 1978) 4:302 (my translation). Hereafter, quotes from Bachmann's collected works, translated by myself, are cited as *Werke*, followed by the appropriate volume and page number.

4 For a discussion of the historical climate surrounding Bachmann's early career, see George C. Schoolfield, "Ingeborg Bachmann," *Essays on Contemporary German Literature*, ed. Brian Keith-Smith (London: Oswald Wolff, 1969) 4:187-212.

5 Sabine I. Gölz. "Reading in Twilight: Canonization, Gender, the Limits of Language − and a Poem by Ingeborg Bachmann," *New German Critique* 47 (1989): 45.

6 See Sara Lennox, "Bachmann and Wittgenstein," *Modern Austrian Literature* 18.3-4 (1985) 239-259.

7 Ludwig Wittgenstein. *Tractatus Logico-Philosophicus*, trans. D.F. Pears and B.F. McGuinness (London: Routledge, 1961) 151. Hereafter referred to as *Tractatus*.

8 *Werke* 4:23.

9 Edgar Marsch. "Ingeborg Bachmann," *Deutsche Dichter der Gegenwart*, ed. Benno von Wiese (Berlin: Erich Schmidt, 1973) 515 (my translation).

10 *Werke* 4:335.

11 See Wolfgang Bender, "Ingeborg Bachmann," *Deutsche Literatur der Gegenwart*, ed. Dietrich Weber (Stuttgart: Kröner, 1976) 585. *Die Scherben*

also means "shards" of glass or pottery. In connection with this meaning, Jo Ann Van Vliet observes that Bachmann's frequent reference to *Scherben* might also echo the glass shards of "Kristallnacht" on November 9, 1938, "as well as the lines of a Hitler Youth anthem: 'Wir werden weiter marschieren/ wenn alles in Scherben fällt/ denn heute gehört uns Deutschland/ und morgen die ganze Welt.'" See her "'Wie alle Glocken schweigen': Guilt and Absolution in Ingeborg Bachmann's 'Psalm,'" *Modern Austrian Literature* 18:3-4 (1985) 125-126.

[12] *Werke* 4:230.

[13] *Tractatus*, 115.

[14] *Tractatus*, 151.

[15] *Werke* 4:27.

[16] See Hans Höller, *Ingeborg Bachmann: Das Werk – Von den frühesten Gedichten bis zum "Todesarten"-Zyklus* (Frankfurt: Athenäum, 1987) 170-190. Höller makes a strong argument that Bachmann's early and late poems are best read together.

[17] *Werke* 2:132.

[18] See Kurt Bartsch, *Ingeborg Bachmann* (Stuttgart: Metzlersche, 1988) 132-133. Bartsch quotes Bachmann's pride in the poem in an unpublished interview from 1973.

[19] Hans Höller. *Ingeborg Bachmann: Das Werk – Von den frühesten Gedichten bis zum "Todesarten"-Zyklus* (Frankfurt: Athenäum, 1987) 171.

[20] *Werke* 4:304.

Fall Down, Heart: "Hymettus" is the name of a mountain that overlooks Athens from the east, and which is famous for its honey and marble.

Reigen: This is also the title of a play by Arthur Schnitzler, written in 1900 and first published in 1921. Causing an uproar in Vienna because of its blatant sexuality, it was subsequently banned. Schnitzler then insisted that the play should not be performed until fifty years after his death, a wish culminated by the first performance given in Vienna by the Akademietheater in 1983.

Borrowed Time: Hans Höller points out a strong echo in this poem with Brecht's "Aus einem Lesebuch fur Städtebewohner" (See Höller, *Ingeborg Bachmann: Das Werk*, 22).

In Twilight: The first line in German makes use of the idiom "die Hände ins Feuer legen," meaning to swear or guarantee that something is true.

Early Noon: Numerous critics have pointed out that stanzas 4 and 5 contain strong echoes of Goethe's lyric "Der König in Thule" from *Faust I*. "Am Brunnen vor dem Tore" is also the first line of Wilhelm Mühler's "Der Lindenbaum," which Schubert set to music in *Die Winterreise*.

Great Landscape Near Vienna: stanza 6 – "Limes" is the name of the system of Roman fortifications along the banks of the Danube which represented the northern defense line of the Roman Empire in present day Austria. Hans Holthusen was the first to observe the similarity between Bachmann's depiction of Vienna in stanza 7 and the portrait of the city in Carol Reed's film, *The Third Man* (See Koschel and Weidenbaum 32). Meanwhile, George Schoolfield astutely observes that the character Orson Welles famously portrays in the film is named Harry Lime, thus rendering a more sinister feel to Bachmann's construction of "Limesgefühl."

Stanza 11 – "Maria am Gestade" is the name of a church located on the banks of the Danube canal in Vienna that is also prominently featured in *The Third Man*.

A Monologue of Prince Myshkin to the Ballet Pantomime "The Idiot": The speaker and all of the characters portrayed are from Dostoevsky's novel *The Idiot*. The basic plot line that Bachmann draws upon is the competition between Prince Myshkin and Parfyon Rogozhin over Nastasya Filippovna, who is eventually murdered by Rogozhin. For a time, Aglaia is also romantically linked to Myshkin, though he ends up rejecting her. Ganya Ivolgin, Totski, and General Epanchin are figures from the Petersburg society that preys upon the well meaning, yet naive Myshkin. It's interesting to note that the one major character not referred to or portrayed by Bachmann is the consumptive idealist, Ippolit.

The composer for the pantomime, Hans Werner Henze, also collaborated with Bachmann on two operas, as well as setting several of her poems to music.

Of a Land, a River and Lakes: The first line of the poem derives from the title of a Grimm fairy tale, "Märchen von einer, der auszog, das Fürchten zu lernen." Bachmann, however, does not follow the plot of the tale in constructing her own mythic tale over the length of the poem.

Section IV, stanza 6 – "Wacholder" is a brand of schnapps.

Invocation of the Great Bear: The bear referred to is that of the Big Dipper constellation, otherwise known as Ursa Major. Here the bear is not only spoken to, but also begins to speak itself at the start of the second stanza.

My Bird: Hans Holthusen was the first to point out that the owl is associated with Athena in Greek mythology, the goddess of wisdom, war, and the arts (See Koschel and Weidenbaum 47).

Curriculum Vitae: "Rose Red" in stanza 2 is a figure from another Grimm fairy tale whose sister's name is Snow White.

The Blue Hour: stanza 3 – "Sternthaler" is a little girl in a Grimm fairy tale by the same name. Having given away her bread, shoes, and dress to others more needy, she becomes rich when she collects the stars falling out of the sky in her slip. "Sternthaler" is also the name of a 19th-century German coin.

Songs from an Island: This poem was set to music by Hans Werner Henze, carrying with it the same title.

In Apulia: The title refers to a region in southeastern Italy.

At Agrigento: Agrigento is a town located in southwestern Italy that is also the site of Greek temples.

Songs in Flight: The epigraph is from Petrarch's "Triumph of Love." Ernest Hatch Wilkins translates the passage as "Hard is the law of Love! but though unjust / One must obey it, for that law prevails / Throughout the universe, and lasts for aye" (*The Triumphs of Petrarch*, Chicago: U of Chicago P, 1962, p.26).

Section III, stanza 1 – The Sporades are a group of Greek islands located in the Aegean Sea.

Section IV, stanzas 2 and 3 – Posilipo and Vomero are hillside regions on the outskirts of Naples. Camaldoli is a mountain just north of Florence.

Section XIV, stanza 1 – The Toledo is the central river of Naples.

Section XV – Holthusen observes the strong link between this section and Rilke's *Sonette an Orpheus*, "1,19" (See Koschel and Weidenbaum 51). Kurt Bartsch also observes a link between "Sinken um uns von Gestirnen" and Robert Musil's play *Die Schwärmer*, which Bachmann helped adapt for the radio (See Bartsch 73)

Hôtel de la Paix: This is the name of a hotel in Paris where Bachmann lived in the fall of 1956.

Aria I: Both this and "Safe Conduct (Aria II)" were set to music by Hans Werner Henze in an orchestral piece titled "Nachtstücke und Arien nach Gedichte von Ingeborg Bachmann."

Bohemia Lies by the Sea: Bachmann refers to Shakespeare's *Love's Labour's Lost* in the third line. The entire poem plays upon *The*

Winter's Tale and the fact that Shakespeare was criticized by Johnson for saying in the play that Bohemia lies by the sea when, in fact, it does not (See Bartsch 132 - 133).

Prague, January '64: The Hradčany is the name of the central square in Prague.

Enigma: Hans Werner Henze's "Ariosi" is a musical setting of poems by Torquato Tasso. Kurt Bartsch points out that "Nichts mehr wird kommen" is a line from the "Peter Altenberglieder" of Alban Berg, while "Du sollst ja nicht weinen" comes from Mahler's Symphony No. 2. (See Bartsch 130).

INGEBORG BACHMANN

A CHRONOLOGY

1926
Birth on June 25 in Klagenfurt, Austria.

1945-50
Study of law, then philosophy at the universities of Innsbruck, Graz, and Vienna. Degree awarded by the University of Vienna in 1950 for a dissertation entitled "The Critical Reception of Martin Heidegger's Existential Philosophy."

1948-49
First poems published in *Lynkeus. Dichtung, Kunst, Kritik*, edited by Hermann Hakel.

1951-53
Scriptwriter at Radio Rot-Weiß-Rot in Vienna.

1952
First reading at the Gruppe 47 gathering. Libretto for the ballet pantomime *The Idiot*, with music by Hans Werner Henze.

1953
Receives the Gruppe 47 Prize. *Die gestundete Zeit*, poetry, published by Frankfurter Verlaganstalt.

1953-57
Lives in Italy on the island of Ischia, in Naples, and in Rome.

1955
Die Zikaden, radio play, produced in Hamburg. Invitation to take part in international seminar at the Harvard Summer School of Arts and Sciences, led by Henry Kissinger.

1956
Anrufung des Großen Bären, poetry, published by R. Piper Verlag, Munich.

1957
Awarded the Bremen Literature Prize.

1957-58
Works as a dramaturge for Bavarian Television and Radio in Munich.

1958
Der gute Gott von Manhattan, radio play, broadcast in Munich and Hamburg.

1958-73
Lives in Zurich and Rome. Involved with the Swiss writer Max Frisch until 1962, after which Bachmann lives primarily in Rome.

1959
Awarded the Radio Play Prize of the War Blind. Delivers acceptance speech entitled "Die Wahrheit ist dem Menschen zumutbar."

1959-60
Invitation to deliver the first lectures for the poetry chair at Frankfurt University. Delivers five lectures concerning "Fragen zeitgenössischer Dichtung."

1960

Libretto for Hans Werner Henze's opera *Der Prinz von Homburg*.

1961

Das dreißigste Jahr, stories, published by R. Piper Verlag, Munich. Awarded the Berlin Critics Prize. Translations of Giuseppe Ungaretti published by Suhrkamp, Frankfurt.

1963

Residence in Berlin with support of Ford Foundation.

1964

Awarded Georg Büchner Prize. Her acceptance speech, *Eine Ort Zufälle*, is later published by Klaus Wagenbuch, Berlin, with thirteen drawings by Günter Grass.

1965

Libretto for Hans Werner Henze's opera *Der junge Lord*.

1968

Awarded the Austrian State Prize for Literature.

1971

Malina, novel, published by Suhrkamp, Frankfurt.

1972

Simultan, stories, published by R. Piper Verlag, Munich. Awarded Anton Wildgans Prize of Society of Austrian Industrialists.

1973

Death in Rome on October 17. Burial in Klagenfurt.

I. WORKS BY BACHMANN

Die gestundete Zeit. Frankfurt: Frankfurter Verlaganstalt, 1953. Munich: Piper, 1957.

Anrufung des Großen Bären. Munich: Piper, 1956.

Der gute Gott von Manhattan. Munich: Piper, 1958.

Das dreißigste Jahr. Munich: Piper, 1961.

Gedichte, Erzählungen, Hörspiel, Essays. Munich: Piper, 1964.

Malina. Frankfurt am Main: Suhrkamp, 1971.

Simultan. Munich: Piper, 1972.

Werke. In 4 Bänden, eds. Christine Koschel, Inge von Weidenbaum, and Clemens Münster. Munich: Piper, 1978.

Frankfurter Vorlesungen: Probleme zeitgenössischer Dichtung. Munich: Piper, 1980.

Die Wahrheit ist dem Menschen zumutbar: Essays, Reden, Kleinere Schriften. Munich: Piper, 1981.

Wir müssen wahre Sätze finden: Gespräche und Interviews, eds. Christine Koschel and Inge von Weidenbaum. Munich: Piper, 1983.

II. WORKS BY BACHMANN IN ENGLISH TRANSLATION

In the Storm of Roses: Selected Poems of Ingeborg Bachmann.
Trans. , ed. , and intro. Mark Anderson. Princeton: Princeton UP, 1986.
The Thirtieth Year. Trans. Michael Bullock. London: Andre
Deutsch, 1964. New York: Holmes & Meier, 1987.
Three Paths to the Lake. Trans. Mary Fran Gilbert. New York:
Holmes & Meier, 1989.
Malina. Trans. Philip Boehm. New York: Holmes & Meier, 1990.
Translation of *Der Fall Franza* and *Requiem für Fanny
Goldmann.* Evanston: Northwestern UP (forthcoming).

III. WORKS ON BACHMANN

Achberger, Karen R. *Understanding Ingeborg Bachmann.*
Understanding Modern European and Latin American Literature,
ed. James N. Hardin. Columbia: U of South Carolina Press, 1994.

Bareiss, Otto, and Frauke Ohloff. *Ingeborg Bachmann: Eine
Bibliographie.* Munich: Piper, 1978.

Bartsch, Kurt. *Ingeborg Bachmann.* Stuttgart: Metzlersche, 1988.

Beicken, Peter. *Ingeborg Bachmann.* Munich: Beck, 1988.

Bender, Wolfgang. "Ingeborg Bachmann," in *Deutsche Literatur der
Gegenwart,* ed. Dietrich Weber. Stuttgart: Kröner, 1976, pp. 584 - 604.

Bürger, Christa. "Ingeborg Bachmann's Emergence from
Aesthetic Modernism." *New German Critique* 47 (1989), 3-28.

Gölz, Sabine I. "Reading in Twilight: Canonization, Gender, the
Limits of Language – and a Poem by Ingeborg Bachmann. *New
German Critique* 47 (1989) 29-52.

Höller, Hans, ed. *Der dunkle Schatten, dem ich schon seit Anfang folge
– Vorschläge zu einer neuen Lektüre des Werkes.* Vienna: Löcker, 1982.

————. *Ingeborg Bachmann: Das Werk – Von den frültesten
Gedichten bis zum "Todesarten"-Zyklus.* Frankfurt: Athenäum, 1987.